THE AFTER

THE

A Veteran's Notes
on Coming Home

AFTER

MICHAEL RAMOS

THE UNIVERSITY OF NORTH CAROLINA PRESS

Chapel Hill

Set in Scala and Univers Next
by Jamison Cockerham

Cover map by the US Geological Survey, Department of the Interior.

Manufactured in the United States of America

LIBRARY OF CONGRESS CATALOGING-IN-PUBLICATION DATA
Names: Ramos, Michael (Michael S.), author.
Title: The after : a veteran's notes on coming home / Michael Ramos.
Other titles: Veteran's notes on coming home
Description: Chapel Hill : The University of North Carolina Press, [2024]
Identifiers: LCCN 2023034105 | ISBN 9781469678078 (paperback ; alk. paper)
   | ISBN 9781469678085 (ebook)
Subjects: LCSH: Ramos, Michael (Michael S.) | United States. Marine Corps.
   Fleet Marine Force—Anecdotes. | Iraq War, 2003–2011—Veterans—Biography.
   | Iraq War, 2003–2011—Veterans—Psychology. | College teachers—North
   Carolina—Biography. | United States—Armed Forces—Chaplain's assistants—
   Biography. | LCGFT: Autobiographies. | Essays.
Classification: LCC DS79.767.V47 R36 2024
   | DDC 956.7044/3 [B]—dc23/eng/20230808
LC record available at https://lccn.loc.gov/2023034105

*For the Marines and sailors I served with and veterans
I have met since leaving active service trying to make
a go of the after. We'll get there one day.*

CONTENTS

COMM CHECK

....

If you're a civilian and you're reading this, before anything else, I want to say thank you. Thank you for reading, thank you for being curious about my experience, and thank you for being someone worth serving for. I appreciate your willingness to explore my experiences with military culture and what it meant to come home. Before we get started, I have three things I want you to know.

I'm not a war hero, I'm not a victim, and I'm not angry at you. As you read these pages, remember these, especially that last one.

I was in the Navy assigned to the Fleet Marine Forces (Marines), what we call a Greensider. Civilians get confused sometimes and just say I was in the Marines. If I was a civilian, I bet I would forget and get that wrong, too. I forget I was a civilian once. To be honest, I have trouble remembering what life before enlisting, before the bang, was like.

I was an RP. Religious Program Specialist is the actual job title, but RP was what my Marines called me most of the time. It's a badge of honor, and all these years later if I hear someone say, "Hey, RP," I still turn my head and smile.

As an RP I worked with US Navy chaplains. Everywhere they go, we go. Ships, stations, with the Fleet Marine Forces. On the Greenside,

RPs were force protection for chaplains because the military's spiritual leaders weren't allowed to carry weapons. So that was part of my job. I say "were force protection" because a still-active RP friend of mine says the job has changed and moved away from warfighting, but that's only what I hear. If I'm being honest, force protection was my favorite part of the job, but there was more to it than shoot 'em up bang bang. I did a lot of admin, too. Like a lot, a lot. The unsexy, uncool stuff like sending in annual reports and answering phones. Other than in passing, I don't talk in this book about my job as an RP or the chaplains I worked with; that is another story for another time. What I do talk about here is as accurate an account as memory allows of what coming home from war was like for me. It's a record of things I saw, heard, and felt *at home.*

This story goes against what we as Americans are taught in school about patriotism. My story also goes against what society—and maybe even you—think our veterans and warriors should feel about wartime experiences and coming home. And I'm good with that because I wrote this for folks like me who did the job the service asked them to and then came home to have a life—only that life was not what any of us were expecting or prepared for. At our seps briefs, they never told us the truth about coming home. From what I hear, they still don't. And I think someone needs to, even if my experience is just one of so many.

I also wrote this story for my Marines and other combat vets who may not ever tell—or be able to tell—their loved ones what coming home from war was like for them. I want them to be able to say, "Hey, this weird little Navy dude knows what it was like, read this and let's talk." I wrote it so folks like me—children of the GWOT—and veterans as a whole would know they aren't alone, and we can talk about what coming home was, and is, really like.

If you're a civilian reader, you might think while reading some of these pages that I'm angry at you. I'm not. Sometimes I'm just being direct. But I *am* angry in parts of my story. About attitudes, about perceptions. At people—military, veterans, civilians. And I have a right to be. Anger is real, and we all have a right to our feelings. Good anger can stir people to action, to make a difference, to protect, to act, to create. Anger can unite and build relationships, which is part of what I hope this book will do for the civilian and veteran communities. On the other hand, rage, like the rage of Achilles, is not okay. Rage is destructive. Rage destroys relationships. I used to be enraged a lot. Especially when I first came home, when I first got out. But when viewed through the lens of relationships, I learned that rage isn't productive or healthy.

You know who taught me that? The people I came home to. By "home," rather than physical or geographic space, I mean the place of relationships and mutual acceptance. The people, in addition to the military and veteran community, who helped me are the civilians I chose as my people. The colleagues I call my friends. Some of my students. All of them thank me for my service and recognize I have conflicting, complicated feelings about it but respect and value me. Other important, supportive people don't thank me for my service (because believe it or not, the thanks isn't compulsory) but value all the good things the military taught me and show me how much they appreciate me. Random civilians have done the same. I learned by watching them, like I watched my senior Marines. I realized some civilians aren't satisfied with canned, trite patriotism, and others didn't assume I was a broken vet with nothing to contribute. And so, since those people thought like me and appreciated me, how could I or why would I be enraged at them and treat them poorly?

So if you're a civilian reader and think I'm angry with you, ask yourself if you're doing the things I call out, like assuming I'm a hero or a victim, or wanting my story to meet your expectations, for example. If these things don't apply to you, then don't worry about it. The same goes for my brother and sister vets, too, because we are not angels or innocent, myself least of all, and some of us are still that asshat vet years after learning better.

Because I wrote this book for people who've served, things I and other veterans consider funny civilian readers may not. I wish I was funny. I think about Ice-T and his rap "Original Gangsta," and how he said that every time he tried to write a rap about partying and good times, like the rappers popular then did, his pen would explode and he found he could only write rhymes about the gangsta life. Sometimes I feel like that when I wish I could write something funny. All that said, if you think something you read here is funny but you aren't sure you have permission to laugh, you do. Laugh. We military folks love to laugh at ourselves and each other. My wife, Lisa, and I were at a party once, and a civilian woman who was a friend of a friend said something like, "Oh you know how crazy those war vets can be," to which Lisa, replied, "No, tell us." And so, the woman did. And then I said, "You do know that we are war vets, right?" I paused for effect. The woman's husband thought she was a goner for sure. Then the woman did the best thing. "Well then, you know what I mean," she said. She paused for effect. My wife and I—both veterans—laughed with her. That is, we laughed together.

Speaking of doing things together—what follows can be tense and intense. It was a hell of a thing to live, even more of a thing to write, so it must be the same to read it. Take a break when you need to. When I wrote this, as I crafted it, I thought a lot about music and art (painting) books and how you can enjoy the whole thing all at once, or piecemeal. I'm serious. Take a break when you need to. I had to take many breaks as I wrote and revised and wrote and revised again, so I won't be offended. It's a lot. A lot to see, hear, feel, and think about. Just pick it back up when you can, so we can think together.

THE AFTER

JUST A MOVIE

....

Did you see *American Sniper*, a student said to me. Yes, I said. What
did you think, she said. I drew a deep breath and stared out the
window.

I think it was a movie, I said. What does that even mean, she said.
I can tell she wants to talk about this, that she has been waiting
for this, though I don't know why. It means that a movie can't get
everything right. Like what, she said. Well, for one the battle was too
clean. No smoke. No dust. No grit. No filth. The uniforms were too
clean and so were the streets. Not enough trash. The Marines weren't
aggressive enough. Marines love battle. They live for it. It sounds
cliché, but that doesn't make it untrue. It just is. The Marines in the
movie were timid, unskilled.

And some of the smaller details. What details, she says. Well, the
spacing is always off, and no one makes jokes in the movies. And the
smell. What smell, she said. Exactly, I said. Movies can't capture the
smell of dirty feet and BO and cordite and mud and trash and blood
and sweat and shit. So, I think it was just a movie, I said.

I think it's not fair how he died, she said. To survive all that to be
killed here at home, she said. That's life, it isn't fair, I said. But didn't
he earn the right to live in peace, she said. I am not sure what she

wants me to say. That's not true. I do know. She wants what everyone wants. For me to say it is unfair and tragic. To feel something. The movies have trained her to want that kind of response even if it isn't warranted. And it isn't some stupid masculine thing or whatever. Because women vets do it, too. Things happen, and in our life, it is what it is.

It isn't fair that one of our guys got killed by a stray bullet in his backyard at his homecoming party, I said. Or that Sam got killed because a cab driver dropped him off at the wrong house, or Jason got killed by his drunk, druggy roommates. Or Gunny Kyle got killed in a motorcycle accident because the other driver was careless. But that doesn't change that it happens, I said.

And it isn't fair that we didn't get killed while so many of our friends did. That it hurts sometimes that we get to go to college, teach classes, get nice jobs, love our wives and children, while our friends who got killed in action or here at home do not.

I didn't say that. I didn't say that because no matter how many times I do it never makes sense to anyone who hasn't been there. It doesn't even make any sense to us half the time. It just is. Instead, I shrug. And turn back to the whiteboard to start the lesson.

PART ONE

BOXES

....

If I die in a combat zone, box me up and ship me home, is how the cadence goes.

This is the box, the CO said at a staff meeting. Marines shouldn't be getting awards if they are operating in the box. The box is big, he said. We don't hand out awards for doing what's in your box, he said. But operating outside the box, thinking outside the box, that gets awarded.

At Navy boot camp, I stand in front of a long table with my issued clothing in a green seabag and a big, empty cardboard box. Take off your shoes, the civilian man says. We take off our shoes. Put them in the box in front of you, he says. We put them in the box. Take off your socks, he says. We take off our socks. Put them in the box. We put them in the box. Put on your issued black socks. We put on our issued black socks. Take off your pants. We take off our pants. Put them in the box. We put them in the box. Take off your skivvies. We look around. What are skivvies? Underwear. We take off our underwear. Put it in the box or in the trash bin. We put our underwear in the box or trash bin. Put on your issued underwear. We put on our issued underwear. Put on your blue sweatpants. We put on our blue sweatpants. Take off your shirt. We take off our shirts. Put them in the box. We put them in the box. If you have a skivvy shirt, take it off.

If we have skivvy shirts, we take them off. Put them in the box. We put them in the box. Put on your white, Navy PT shirt. We put on our white, Navy PT shirt. Put on your blue sweat top. We put on our blue sweat tops. Take the flaps of the box and fold them down. We take the flaps of the box and fold them down. Pick up the marker in front of you. We pick up the marker in front of us. Write your name in all caps on the first line of the To box. We write our names in all caps on the first line of the box. Write your address in all caps on the next line in the To box. We write our addresses on the next line in all caps. Write your city, state, and zip code in all caps on the last line of the To box. We write our city, state, and zip codes on the last line of the box. Close the box. We close the box. Someone will come by and tape your box shut. Someone comes by and tapes our boxes shut. Our RDCs come for us, take us away from our boxes.

We stand in boxes. Formation they call it. But it's a box. A box of people in rank and file. Our boxes are mobile. We can face left, face right, face about, forward march pass in review past the dignitary box all in our boxes marching we march to schools to duty stations.

At my first duty station I take custody of the mount-out box. I am an RP at 1st CEB 1 MARDIV. I guard and assist the chaplain. By guard, I mean he doesn't carry a weapon, I do. A bodyguard, a bullet sponge. By assist, I mean answer phones, take out trash, walk around the battalion, go to the field, set up religious services, and take responsibility for the mount-out box. The mount-out box is a seven-cube, a box with seven cubic feet of space. The mount-out box has a packing list, prescribed by senior RPs and other officers in Washington. The seven-cube had: a thirty-day supply of wine—kosher and sacramental—prayer cards, prayer beads, rosary beads, Bibles, Korans, Torahs, Armed Forces Hymnals, candles, communion hosts, and grape juice. I had to waterproof the box to protect the contents from flooding when we put the box on a ship and the ship gets flooded or when it comes off a cargo plane and it's raining wherever the Marine Corps has sent us. The seven-cube held everything my battalion needed to sustain its religious needs for thirty days. Thirty is the magic number. We planned on not being resupplied for thirty days at our level.

I think Regiment's box, the next up the chain, was a sixty-day box. Division's box was ninety days. All with the same stuff, just in larger quantities. My seven-cube was a green wooden heavy box with a heavy-duty lock.

The lock was to protect the wine from unauthorized consumption even though sacramental wine was almost undrinkable. I learned to pack only what our Marines needed and not what the list from Washington said I had to have. I had two boxes. One for the inspection, when someone from Division came to make sure my box matched the official list, and the real box, the one I took to Iraq. One day someone from S-4 told everyone to pack their boxes and mark them for embark. I was already packed. Someone from the 4 came and got my box and put it in a bigger box, a QUADCON or a PALCON maybe. I never saw it until we got to Kuwait. My box was waiting for me. I dragged that box all over Iraq. I kept an inventory of the box in my notebook. Sometimes I slept on the box.

Other times we slept in boxes dug into the ground. One-man fighting positions, Ranger graves, graves. No one used the fancy names. Just graves or holes. The boxes were dug deep enough for us to lie in at night and to protect us from IDF. The boxes also had the benefit of being ready-made holes in case we got killed, we all joked.

Sometimes in Iraq we would get priority mailboxes. Magic. These boxes can take a group of rough, tough, combat-hardened Marines tired, hungry, and dirty from killing and protecting each other and turn them into excited, energized little boys because they got mail. It's easy to forget that most of them are still boys. Teenagers, a few not even eighteen, many not even twenty-one, carrying weapons and the burden of killing a man and protecting his buddy and some had the extra burden of leading and making decisions that could get a guy killed even if they are the right decisions. But mailboxes helped make you forget all that for a second.

Small and white with red and blue stripes, priority mailboxes brought fresh socks, snacks, smokes, pictures of home, and, if we were lucky, soft toilet paper. Oftentimes doting moms and loving wives would send extra items in the boxes because they knew we shared with everyone around us. Fun fact: those boxes smelled like home. It's easy to forget what home smells like when all you smell is sand and BO and blood and sweat and ball stink and trash. It's easy to forget home when you have a job to do and that job requires you to wear a flak and Kevlar and carry a weapon with you all the damn time even to the shitter which could be a plastic box or sometimes be a hole you'd dug.

I handed out dozens of those boxes. People would send us boxes addressed to Any Marine. But I never gave them to Any Marine. I gave them to my Marines. It was cool to get a box from a random American. Mostly because we wanted what was in it but also because it meant that people back home cared. This was early when the war was cool and America was pissed about the Towers and you could choke a whole city with all the yellow ribbons. Random folks sent us socks, snacks, and smokes, too. We sometimes wrote thank-you notes back to the people who sent us boxes.

I used to look forward to getting boxes from my son filled with his schoolwork or art and the occasional handwritten note. We were supposed to burn all that stuff to protect us and our families if we were captured or tortured, of course, but I liked getting his boxes anyway. I didn't and I don't recall anyone burning mail from home unless we just couldn't carry it. When you live off what you can cram in a pack or on your back, you have to make choices. One time the day we were leaving Iraq and a few hours before I almost killed a man at a VCP to protect my chaplain and my Marines, one of the guys from 2nd CEB got a box and we were standing in a box bull-shitting waiting for Gunny and we didn't see him walk up on us and Gunny does that sometimes, sneak up on you, and since we didn't seem to notice that he was there for box time—formation—he yelled Ah-ten-hut. And we all snapped to attention and the poor Marine who had just gotten a box and was holding it dropped the box and the contents went everywhere and got covered in that powdery shitty sand that probably has a ton of chemicals that are slowly killing us now.

Even our shitters were boxes. So were our showers. Shitters were only when we were at a base or camp, otherwise we used a cat hole or straddle trench. Unless of course you had an ammo box, that was a luxury shitter. And showers, those were at bases and camps, too. When we left Kuwait and shitter and shower boxes, I think I had like five showers maybe. One from a busted pipe and two from a bucket that we put holes in and zip-tied to the top of a Humvee while someone stood on the Humvee and poured water through the bucket. Okay, maybe I only had three showers.

Our food came in boxes. The actual meals came in bags, which had boxes in them. But the bags came in boxes. Somewhere, for some reason, we stopped getting resupplied with boxes of MREs. We were down to one meal a day, which wasn't enough. The boxes that individual components came in made excellent postcards to send home. I sent a few home. I told my wife and son I was fine and the postcard was proof that I was eating and fine.

When the fighting stopped and we were all—we being most of First Marine Division—at Diwaniyah they brought us hot food in green mermite boxes. It wasn't great, but it beat MREs and it beat starving. We all got the shits in Diwaniyah.

We really do box people up and ship them home if they die in a combat zone, just like the cadence says. Before Marines get boxed up, the truth is, sometimes their Marines have to go collect the parts of their buddies and put them in bags so they can be shipped to the rear to be boxed up in a nice coffin and covered with a flag. Then some Marine, or maybe a Doc or an RP who was also friends with that Marine has to go and box up and inventory the belongings of the Marine who got killed. The box the Marine goes in gets covered in an American flag and then that box gets lowered into the ground while "Taps" plays and moms and wives and little brothers and dads and sisters sob.

Sometimes we might have tears, too. I don't like to think about how many people I know in boxes and how many boxes I have seen lowered into the ground. I hate those boxes.

These things sound outrageous and horrible. They are all within the box the CO mentioned earlier.

Even when I got home from Iraq, during PT, I would sing, If I die in a combat zone, box me up and ship me home. We all did. Even after all of that.

After nine years, ten months, and twenty-eight days, I left the military. TMO came and packed my everything into boxes. TMO took an inventory of my stuff and then put it in a larger box to ship it to my new home. When I got to my new place, my stuff was not waiting for me. When the movers came, they unpacked everything and took all their boxes with them.

I am a civilian now. Those boxes—the seven-cubes and ammo can shitters and mailboxes and coffins—seem like forever ago, and sometimes I can still feel and smell those boxes. For a while I was sending boxes to my son when he lived in California and I in North Carolina. It wasn't a war zone, but divorce isn't easy. When he was young, I used to fill his boxes with Legos, his favorite snacks, and a handwritten note.

I am a civilian now. My journal, a Bible, uniforms, boots, medals, ribbons, MRE postcards, some shrapnel, an Iraqi compass, service record, awards are all in a box in my closet under bags and other things. I never open the box those things are in.

My son enlisted in the Marine Corps. Soon, he will box his stuff up and send it home. He will sing about being boxed up and shipped home if he dies in a combat zone. He will get mailboxes, and he might have to collect his friends' body parts and box up his friends' stuff. He could come home in a box. Or he could not. Maybe when he is older he will write about the boxes he sent me and the boxes I sent him as a kid and how those boxes differed from the ones I sent him when he was a Marine.

HAZELNUT

Sergeant Major, can I ask you a question, I said. Sure, RP, he said. Sergeant Major Ellis grabbed a white foam cup, grabbed the powdered hazelnut creamer, and dumped maybe a half inch of creamer into the cup before pouring the coffee I brewed every morning. He came to have coffee with me every morning, or rather he came to get the coffee I brewed in my office at battalion and he might ask how my libo was or how the Marines were or maybe even how I was doing, but generally he just returned my greeting and took his cup of coffee after chipping in some cash for the mess. This was in Oki in 2005, when I was an RP2 and Fox company office was next door to mine and SSgt Cardenas a Fox platoon sergeant came and chitchatted and grabbed coffee, black with the occasional bit of powdered creamer, every morning, and SSgt Poole the Marines' Career Jammer—they hate that by the way, Career Retention Specialist is the official, preferred term—came to chitchat and get coffee, black, or if it was a little strong a dash of creamer, and First Sergeant Carlson from H&S came and chitchatted and got coffee, black, every morning. Not Sergeant Major, though, he took it with cream—he even told me to make sure I stocked plenty of hazelnut creamer in my coffee mess for him, which I did. And of course, being a good Sergeant Major he made sure he donated money to the coffee mess fund so me being junior didn't have to come out of pocket for seniors.

Sergeant Major, I said, you're a combat vet battalion Sergeant Major Force Recon jump and dive pins PT beast, so what gives with the froufrou hazelnut creamer. He looked at me with that look he gave when he sized you up and made decisions about how to approach you like we all do and learned from senior Marines like him for a moment while he stirred his coffee. He waited for a second before answering, and he said, RP, I am a combat vet battalion Sergeant Major Force Recon jump and dive pins PT beast, I can have my coffee any way I want, and if I want froufrou hazelnut creamer in my coffee I will have it without questions from you RP, you gotta fucking problem with that. No, Sergeant Major, I said, just wondering. Thanks for the coffee RP, he said and walked out to do Sergeant Major things, which were way above my RP things.

A few years later, in '08, after Sergeant Major Ellis got killed in Barwanah on the pump I missed in '07, I was an in a staff meeting at the Naval Academy. The Academy was fancy, and we wore service uniforms with ribbons, not cammies like we did when I was with the Marines. One of the chaplains, the Rabbi, she sat next to me and before the O-6 showed up we chitchatted over coffee. As I drank my coffee, she looked over at my cup and sniffed. RP1, she said, can I ask you a question? Yes ma'am, I said. Is that hazelnut creamer, she said. Yes ma'am, it is, I said. I have to say, I am kind of surprised that you don't take it black, I mean you are Iraq War vet RP1 (FMF) Ramos from First Marine Division, so what's with the creamer? Ma'am, I said, I am Iraq War vet RP1 (FMF) Ramos from First Marine Division, and if I want froufrou hazelnut creamer in my coffee, I think I've earned it, is that okay with you, ma'am? I laughed a little and smiled and she smiled and we went on with our meeting.

I take my coffee black now, not because I am a badass or anything, but because I am old and with age comes fat and skipping creamer is a way to cut sugar, plus most of the TAs at the university I lecture at drink it black and it's just easier, still I can't help but smile whenever I smell hazelnut creamer. I still hear his voice all these years later, and I remember the lesson.

SECTION 60,
GRAVE 8356

The stillness is not disconcerting. Adults walk with slow steps up from the subway stop, the parking garage. Children do not laugh or run but mimic the adults. The sounds of the city? What city? There is only the cemetery. The noiselessness accented by the mass of silent Americans filing into the visitor's center.

Off-white walls and soft white light. A kiosk. Paintings and a model of the grounds overwhelming. Daunting. In quiet tones, people say: I am looking for my grandfather, my uncle, my cousin, my father, my mother, my brother. Can you help me? A coordinate is given. A slip of paper. Section number, grave number. Here is who you are looking for. Walk outside, start the journey, find the white marble marker.

Some people come without marble markers to visit. To see them anyway. Because they think they should. There is no sin or judgment for it. Glenn Miller, George Patton, Joe Louis, Audie Murphy, Jackie Cooper, Jackie O. Perhaps they come for the attractions. The Netherlands Carillon and tulips, John F. Kennedy's eternal flame, Robert E. Lee's home. McClellan Gate, the Marine Corps Monument. The Tomb of the Unknown Soldier.

The Tomb. White marble patrolled by soldiers in dress uniform, the Old Guard. Third Infantry Regiment. Blue trousers, black coat, black cover, rifle. Slow ceremonial march. Left foot, right foot, swing that arm, rifle tight, back straight, head and eyes front, gaze unseeing, seeing everything. The crowd, the silence. Stop. Heel click, pivot. Heel click, pivot. White-gloved hand salute. About face. Sound off. About face. White-gloved hand salute. Right face. Heel click, pivot. Forward march.

The clip-clop of a horse-drawn caisson. Soldiers, sailors, airmen, Marines marching. Escorting. A flag-draped casket. Time ceases. Silence. The caisson and casket pass. Old-timers and not-so-old-timers salute. Out of habit. Out of memory. Out of respect. Good night, comrade. We have the watch.

The grass around the white marble marker is green. Too green. The white marble, too white. Few come to this section. No famous people rest here. There are no birds, no squirrels. A jet streaks silent across the sky. Over there, a few rows back and to the right a Marine he served with. Over there, several stones to the left, another. Next to him, a young man whose end date is the same as his. And here, in front of me, lies Joseph J. Ellis, Sergeant Major, US Marine Corps, Sep 8 1966, Feb 7 2007, Purple Heart, Operation Iraqi Freedom.

In that first moment in front of him, I envy those who come only to see the Netherlands Carillon and tulips, John F. Kennedy's eternal flame, Robert E. Lee's home, General McClellan's Gate, the Marine Corps Monument, the Tomb of the Unknown Soldier, Glenn Miller, George Patton, Joe Louis, Audie Murphy, Jackie Cooper, Jackie O., but not their Sergeant Major. And then I don't envy them.

Joseph J. Ellis, Sergeant Major, US Marine Corps. Joe, JJ. Sergeant Major. My Sergeant Major. A Marine's Marine. The man who let my child swing from his arms, who let Filipino children play around his legs, who called Brian Cassidy, whom we called Vito, Bee Sting, after Cassidy, or Vito, almost died twice from a bee sting. The man who didn't yell at me, even though I knew better than to wear shower shoes to the chow hall, but yelled fifty yards across a parade deck to tell two Marines to be quiet during an award ceremony. The man who only cried once when some POG Marine said he was only a Marine until 1630. The man who swept the sand of Iraq out of his hooch. And swept. And swept.

1966. 1976. Only ten years between his year and mine. A decade. Half a generation. Nothing.

Feb 7 2007. Today, May 23 2008. I wait for something. A lesson, a feeling. Something. Anything. Nothing comes.

Rifle fire from a funeral. Taps. I come to attention. Instinct. Habit. Automatic.

Sergeant Major says nothing to me, but I hear his voice. No. I remember its timbre. Sense the vibration in his baritone. I see him punch me to celebrate an award; the force drives the medal's pins into my chest, me in to the wall. I see him shake my hand, crush it. I see him mix his coffee with froufrou hazelnut creamer. I see him do these things, and other things, but I do not hear, do not feel. And neither does he. That is the lesson.

I rise from the knee I bowed without knowing. Remove the hand from the cool of the marble I can't remember touching. Back step. Feet together. Hands at my side. Back straight, head and eyes front, gaze unseeing, seeing everything. Right face, walk away.

WAR STORIES

....

In the middle of the Pacific floating home on the *Bonhomme Richard* in a room the size of a closet we went to Warrior Transition Briefs and tell your stories is what they told us. There were two of them. The woman was gorgeous, at least we thought so, of course we hadn't seen or heard or smelled a woman in months and she could have been a stateside six but to us she was a deployment nine easy. I think she was old, too, forty or something. But hey who cared? None of us had seen our wives or girlfriends in months. Tell your stories, she said to us. We were nice to her because we thought she was pretty.

But the other one, the old man—also about forty, who had a crew cut and an old man belly and one of those khaki fishing vests told us he was a warrior just like us to build rapport and we laughed at him with his crew cut and old man belly. What war did you fight in because we just fought in Iraq, I said. I am a reserve officer, a SWO aboard a cruise missile ship, he said. Oh, I said. Did you fire any of those missiles into Iraq because that's kinda cool. I saw what a bunch of those did to a military base and a military academy and hospital and a school, I said. No, he said. Oh, I said.

Tell your stories to your wife, to your family, to people who will listen because it's important to tell them, and the folks back home want to know, crew cut old man belly said in the briefs. One of the Marines from Charlie company a Mexican kid from probably Texas but maybe Arizona or LA stood up. He knife-handed reserve SWO warrior crew cut old man belly and said, Fuck you I'm not telling my wife anything. She doesn't want to hear about that shit, she doesn't need to hear it and I don't want to tell her, I don't ever want to talk about this, what good will it do, so you and your fucking training can suck my dick. And he walked out. The rest of the Marines followed, he was a Lance Corporal. The NCOs laughed and walked out, too. Catch you at chow RP, Catch you later RP, they said. See you gents, I said.

I looked at crew cut old man belly and deployment nine and shrugged. Well, what'd you expect, I said. The ship was pitching and rolling, though the *Bonhomme Richard*, being a big deck amphib, shouldn't have been moving in the water like that, but that part of the ocean in the middle of nowhere somewhere between Australia and America is pretty rough and we all swayed with the rocking of the ship and I stared at them and they looked at me and tried to convince me of the value of the training in helping us move forward. I shrugged again. I know why you're here, I said. But they aren't gonna tell those stories and they definitely aren't gonna tell those stories to you and they sure as hell aren't gonna tell them to family back home. I appreciate what you're trying to do for us, but this isn't working, I said. It's a waste of time, even if DoD says we have to come to these trainings, I said.

Deployment nine and crew cut old man belly didn't get it. Why not, they said. We've flown onto dozens of ships after deployment and done these briefs hundreds of times and the people aboard responded well, they said. Those people hadn't been to war, I said. Those people hadn't had to kill other people or almost been killed themselves. Things are different now, I said. They respect you and trust you, they said. I'm one of them, I said. And I don't tell them to tell their stories, I said, because I know their stories already.

At random hours of the night a Marine would come to my coffin rack, I had the bottom bunk, and they would ask if I was asleep and if I wanted to go to Midrats, and I was asleep and I didn't want to go to Midrats, but I got up every time and got dressed and we walked around the ship and sometimes they talked and when they did, I listened. But I'm not going to tell you what we talked about. Those stories? Those are ours. We tell them to each other in the darkness or daylight over a beer or whiskey or a case of beer and a bottle of whiskey—and not because we are broken, that's just who we are—and laugh because some of that shit is funny, like the time I saw Metzger shaving his ears because Staff Sergeant Schmidt said his ears were hairy and that was unauthorized or when Ijames and Metzger were in a truck and an RPG hit them but didn't detonate, just kinda went through the windshield and out the back of the Humvee instead. Other times at other stories we don't laugh because it isn't funny. Sometimes we laugh anyway because what else can you do? But those stories? Those stories are for us. For the ones who know and understand and can be silent.

That's the problem with war movies and war stories, they're always so poignant and some symbolic thing happens and everyone's always fucking talking, being deep. Only in those moments, the talking isn't the thing. Because what do you say when it should have been you but wasn't? What do you say when you're older—say fortyish—and have old man belly but no crew cut and sometimes you forget where you are and you think you're back in the sand and you can feel your rifle at your side and the salt on your cammies and smell the diesel and trash and sweat and sand? What do you say to a man who might be just a boy who knew he was safe when he could piss on the side of the road without being afraid of being blown up?

You say nothing because maybe you were that man who was a boy who was too entranced by the beauty of a Spectre gunship at dusk circling slow overhead dropping lume and bombs and firing that bigass cannon on targets just over the berm in Nasiriyah. Maybe you were the boy that was a man who thought the Spectre gunship circling and the dark silhouette of mortars coming down in the pink-orange sunset and the bright white-and-blue flash was gorgeous and didn't know enough to get down when the dust puffed and hot metal went flying. You say nothing because you know in your bones what it's like to have to deliver the news to some of your buddies that one of your guys is gone and later you go to funerals and hear the cries and see the tears of family members in the heat of the day while the grass is green and growing and the bugler is bugling and the sun is rising and setting and the rifle detail is firing and the casket is lowering and that family member is sobbing and the weight of the uniform and ribbons and tradition is heavy. You say nothing because you've heard the snap of a bullet and felt the wind moving faster than you knew air could move and gotten cut on the cheek when one bullet hits a rock and the rock hits your face as the bullet maybe meant for your face misses and you know the surge of adrenaline and the burn in your blood and the rage over someone trying to kill you and the contradictory calm exhilaration because they failed. And you say nothing because you have seen a man, men, and children, too, in your iron sights and know what comes next if you keep squeezing that trigger.

But all of that was a lifetime ago, which is such a cliché thing to say, but it is. And now years removed from all that, after once telling your ex-wife a story about Iraq and her looking at you like you were a monster and not getting it, you only tell stories to the Marines you know and trust and they only tell you the stories that you already kinda know because they trust you.

And still outsiders ask you to tell your stories and you can't help wonder why they want to know about those things. Or if they really want to know about those things, to understand them, to understand you, or so they can get the war without going to war. Because that's pretty common. I once wrote a piece that had one scene with Sergeant Bear giving me his death letter and me taking it and that being the important thing, that in our twenties we were thinking about death and that he trusted me to deliver his final words and I loved him enough to do it. After reading the entire piece, all people wanted to know was if Bear died. And the rare times people do ask me to talk about the war, they usually tell me about their friends' or relatives' stories to try and relate, or they tell some other story from their civilian life to try and relate, or tell me they'd almost joined but, or tell me how intense whatever story I am telling is, or, my favorites, they try to talk politics with me about it, or say, I understand but, or ask how messed up or broken I am. Or how ashamed I must be.

So no, I don't usually tell war stories because most people won't understand—won't being a choice—or maybe they can't, because here where everyone is so far from death, everything is so polite and civilized and we vets are so uncivilized. Our speech and actions don't mesh with everyone else's, and rather than being judged or called racist or misogynist or whatever else, we won't tell our war stories for the sake of telling stories.

BOOTS

I wore Doc Marten eight-holes to boot camp. They were broken in, made in England, and my favorite boots. Before I enlisted thirteen days before 9/11, and every day before that, I wore those boots. At boot camp they made me take my Doc Martens and clothes and pack them in a cardboard box, write my home address in all caps on the box, and send them home. Nine weeks later, after graduation, I asked my wife for my Docs. She'd thrown my civvies and my boots away, she said. They smelled awful, she said.

At Navy boot camp they issued me boondockers to go with my utilities. The utility uniform is: light blue work shirt, navy blue trousers, and black boondockers. Ankle-high black boots that don't have to be polished to a high shine. At Field Med, I went to the PX and couldn't find my way back to the Staff NCO Club on Lejeune, where me and a bunch of other boots had been dropped to take an advancement exam. If I couldn't get back I would be UA. UA meant unauthorized absence, which meant trouble. No one wanted to be UA. I found a guy who had on the same uniform as me. He looked older and senior. I followed him around the store until he turned around. And then I saw his nametag, which was different than mine. He was the air conditioner repairman. A civilian. I hated that uniform and couldn't wait for my Marine issue—cammies and combat boots.

A few months before 9/11, I went to the Marine recruiting office. I wanted to be a Marine. An infantry Marine. But this was before the war when they didn't need infantry Marines. They needed other Marines, so I joined the Navy instead. The recruiter promised me I could volunteer to go with Marines and even learn to fight like one. I only had to be a bodyguard for a chaplain. A Religious Program Specialist, they called it—RP for short, I'd learn. Sold.

Three hours after the attacks on 9/11, after I watched the second plane slam into the Tower and watch people jump from the Tower into I don't know what as I stood dripping wet in a towel asking what movie my wife was watching, before I understood we'd been attacked, I called the recruiter.

Can I get out of my contract, I said. You too, he said. Yes, me too, I said. Everybody wants out of their contracts now, he said. I want to join the Marines, I said. The Navy was my second choice and I'm pretty sure they'll need infantry Marines now, I said. My recruiter laughed. No, he said, you can't get out of your contract. All morning people have been trying to get out of their contracts so they don't go to war, he said. Can I leave early then, I said. No, he said. I hung up. I went to Navy boot camp October 23. And got issued the utility uniform that looked like the air conditioner repairman's and not like a military uniform. But then after volunteering for FMF duty at RP "A" school in Mississippi, I got cammies and combat boots.

My first pair of combat boots were the black leather jungles I got at Field Med with my cammies. Those boots looked sharp, military. Black laces, black treads, black nylon, no dog tag in the left boot. In those days, Marines put a dog tag in their boots only if they were deploying and deployments were scarce and if you were being deployed you were a badass and the envy of everyone else. In the days before war, Marines judged another Marine's motivation by how well he shined his boots. Just blackening them wasn't good enough. You had to have that Marine spit shine or else. I wasn't a Marine, I was a sailor, but that didn't matter. Everyone polished his boots. Except for shitbirds. Shitbirds made excuses. Our company Gunny,

Gunnery Sergeant Jennings, used to tell us that if we had time to sleep we had time to polish our boots—a subtle lesson. I was a boot. I didn't get it. Marines had to tell me that a Marine takes care of his weapon first, his gear second (including boots), then himself. The individual always came last.

On Sundays, the ritual went like this: get a haircut—a high reg or high and tight if you were a boot and/or moto (I was both)—press and starch the cammies, polish the boots. I spent hours on my boots. Once when my son was a toddler he wanted to play, but I was buffing my boots to a high-gloss shine. He stomped his shoes down on my boots to get my attention. I did not play with my son. I repolished my boots.

I learned how to be a killer in those boots. I wore them to the rifle range, where I learned to shoot dog targets, paper targets. Silhouettes of a man lying down, holding a weapon, ready to kill me and my friends, the range NCOs said. It's hard to kill a human, easy to shoot a target, they said. The range coaches tell you to fire when your TARgets appear. See the target, pull the trigger. Easy. Automatic. I got good at shooting targets. Even from 500 yards. The range NCOs had never shot at or killed another human. It isn't as easy as they said.

Do you know what it's like to know that you can hit a human from 200, 300, and even 500 yards? How easy it will be to hit a human closer than that? Did you know that after that moment, if you even have that realization, it doesn't bother you. That it's just the job and you shrug and you forget until a civilian says how intense or terrifying that is, how they could never do that.

I used to run in those boots. Up in the morning with the California sun we ran all day until the running was done. In black jungle boots and cammie bottoms we ran First Sergeant Hill chanting cadences that praised our warrior life, gloried in the blood and guts of it all and regulated our breathing.

We ran two or three miles depending on who was leading us to First Sergeant Hill. It was steep and tall. The path was rocky. Two ropes hung down one side of First Sergeant Hill. The steepest side. With the Staff NCOs shouting encouragement at us we climbed the ropes to the top of the hill. Hand over hand. Quick. With a purpose. Nonchalance was not tolerated. Nonchalance would get you killed. It would get your Marines killed. Marines and Greenside sailors like me were not authorized to get ourselves or anyone else killed.

On one of those rope runs I rolled my right ankle just before the Hill. A Gunny from Supply saw me roll it and said I should take it easy. Maybe I should get in the truck, he said. I said nothing. I tightened my boot. I kept running. I grabbed the rope when it was my turn and climbed to the top of the Hill like everyone else and then ran the two miles back to our headquarters. I didn't think about my ankle. The enemy doesn't care about a rolled ankle. The enemy would kill my friends if I was weak. I refused to be weak.

In those black jungle boots, I learned MCMAP. Marine Corps Martial Arts. Hand-to-hand combat. My sparring partner was Josh Stover. He was a Corporal from the hills of Virginia that bordered Tennessee and spoke with the most pronounced twang I had ever heard. I was a Third Class Petty Officer and had lived in Southern California my whole life. We were in the same company and best friends. My son and his little girl used to play together. He and his wife, and me and mine, once cooked Thanksgiving dinner together, then Stover and I drove to the barracks to find Marines staying alone to invite them to my house and have a family meal. One of those Marines was a kid named Wiscowiche, whom we called Whiskey. Thanks, RP, but I am going home, he said. Where is home, I said. Victorville, he said. I enlisted from Victorville, I said. I used to live on Seneca Road, I said. Me too, he said, in those single-story apartments across from Summer Breeze. No shit, I said, I used to live in Summer Breeze apartments, I said. Whiskey died in Iraq a couple years after that.

Part of MCMAP, besides taking the heel of those black boots and driving it though the skull of my enemy once I had broken his arm or leg or incapacitated him in some other way, was body hardening. Stover and I would get in our basic warrior stance and then kick, punch, or elbow each other's key nerves. The object was to make us immune to pain.

When I first started training with him, Stover used to tell me to hit him harder. I was afraid at first, reluctant to hurt my friend. One time, after a few weeks of training, he lay on his back, me on top of him, elbowing his femoral nerves, he had to tell me to not hit him so hard. I'm not gonna be able to walk, he said.

Josh and I were supposed to go to war together and come home together. But we didn't. He got transferred to a different unit and in an ambush in Nasiriyah he jumped out of a seven-ton and rolled his ankle. He got medevaced. Then he got discharged. Athletes who break their ankles like that never play their sport again, the docs told him.

One day before Josh and I got separated, I got told to go to supply to get TAP gear—desert cammies and desert combat boots. They told me to put a dog tag in my left boot. We were going to Kuwait and, if things went sideways, to Iraq. Do you know what it's like to volunteer with an idea of war, the risk, then walk down to supply to face it? Do you know that pit in your stomach, that hollowness, that watching it happen to someone-elseness? And do you know the thrill of it? The this is it, what we've trained for of it? That the pit of the stomach thing goes away, and you just can't wait to go because this is the job and the life you volunteered for?

My desert combat boots were like the black jungles, only tan, so that they would blend in with the miles and miles and miles of powdery sand and dust.

I practiced breaching and clearing houses and fighting in a gas mask in those boots in the Kuwaiti desert. Once, after teaching me how to call for CAS and fire support, Sergeant Bear, whom we called Bear, asked me to give his death letter to his wife. You don't have to say anything to her, he said. Then he made a just-send-it motion with his hand. Bear was twenty-three. I was twenty-six. Do you know what that's like? To be that young and have your life ahead of you but realizing this is the job you volunteered for so get over it, make peace with it? It makes you old being that young. I stared at his letter in the dark Bedouin tent. I didn't want that letter. I took the letter. I put it in my right cargo pocket and kept it there. What happens if I get killed with his letter, I wondered.

I wore those desert combat boots all over Iraq. I didn't take them off very much. Except to change my socks. I slept in them. I was wearing those boots when I gave Bear his letter back when we got on ship to go home. I was wearing those boots when our battalion XO, Major Jernigan, told us on the flight deck of the *Bonhomme Richard* that who we were as Marines, as warriors, as brothers would be forever tattooed on our souls. He didn't point out that I was a sailor and different. My boots looked like every Marine's boot next to me. Those boots smelled rotten. I threw them overboard the first chance I got.

When I got back from Iraq, I got back into black boots and jungle cammies. I got put on LIMDU for a bad hip. Major Jernigan and the battalion staff fought to keep me, I was theirs, they said. I couldn't leave, they said. But the Navy said I had to go. I'd been hurt and couldn't hump or run. Useless to the Navy and Marine Corps. I got sent where broken and useless people go. Do you know what it's like to be told you're broken and useless after being a part of a team, a family, having a place and a role?

They took away my black combat boots and cammies. They put me in the air conditioner repairman suit again. I was angry. I was sad. I wanted my cammies and combat boots. I wanted to go back to my Marines. A group of nonrated sailors, also in air conditioner repairman suits, asked me if it was true. All the horrible things they heard about Marines. About sleeping at attention and always getting yelled at. We heard that E-4s, NCOs, I corrected them, were bossy and yelled a lot if things didn't get done. I laughed at them. Didn't answer. I saw some First Class Petty Officers getting ready to swab a deck while I, a Third Class, got asked ridiculous questions. What are you doing, I said to the First Classes. Getting ready to swab the deck, they said.

Chief said it had to be done. We have a list of other shit that's gotta get done, too. You are First Classes, I said. You don't swab decks. I don't swab decks as a Third Class, I said. Give me the list. Go do First Class things. I got this. I will make the nonrates do it. After forty-eight hours of me yelling and ordering subordinates around, the Navy in San Diego decided I should go back to the Marines and sailors at Camp Pendleton. They had made a mistake, they said. So sorry, they said. You don't belong here, they said. Leave, they said. So I did.

I got back in cammies and laced up my combat boots—dog tag still in the left boot. Every Marine and sailor was required to have one of his dog tags laced into the left boot now because deployments weren't rare after the Invasion. We were all being deployed, preparing to deploy, or coming back from being deployed so we could do it all over again.

Once, before all that, when I was a boot and had just been issued my boots, I asked why some Marines and Corpsmen we had seen laced dog tags in their left boots. No matter what happens to the Marine, Staff Sergeant Weigman said, blown up, shot up, whatever, the left boot always survives, he said. Since the dog tag has your name and social on it, identifying your mangled, vaporized body is easy. The religious preference is there so the chaplain knows what kind of burial to give you. In case you're dead and can't be asked, he said. Years later, I would give that explanation to my boots when they asked about the dog tag in their boots.

The Marine Corps did away with the black leather boot in 2004. They adopted a new boot, representative of the changing face of warfare, they said. These boots were tan and suede. They didn't need polishing. The Eagle, Globe, and Anchor—the emblem of the Marine Corps—was stamped into the heels. They didn't look as sharp as my old black boots, but they were more comfortable and I got used to them.

I wore those boots on deployment to Okinawa, the site of the last battle of the Pacific Campaign of WWII. I marched in those boots over ground Marines and sailors of my division, the First Marine Division, bled and died on sixty years before I was there.

It rained a lot on Oki. It once rained for nineteen days of a twenty-one-day field op. It was miserable. I had never seen so much or such intense rain. The savage raindrops pelted our bodies all the time. Neither waterproof sleeping bags nor shelters constructed of tied-together ponchos protected us from the rain. We didn't use tents. Infantry Marines were tougher than rain, the officers said. The pounding rain filled our armpit-deep fighting holes in minutes. The red Okinawan clay turned to viscous, tomato soup–colored mud. My boots were always soaked. It was hot and humid. Our skin was always pruned. Many of us got prickly heat. We chafed and bled under our flaks. I chafed and bled. Anyway.

My boots had Okinawan red clay on them for months after that deployment. The clay of Okinawa is like the sand of Iraq. It gets everywhere and into everything. You can't get rid of it.

I wore those boots on my last hump in the infantry. We humped to build our strength and endurance for combat. My last hike in the infantry was supposed to be a twelve-mile easy stroll. It turned into a sixteen-mile combat patrol in full pack.

Up in the morning before the California sun. At 0445 to be exact. March to the armory. Wait in line. Draw weapons. March to the grinder. Put on the pack. Step off. Forward march. In silence. In the dark. After humping the first three miles the column took a break. The Marines did. The Corpsmen, chaplain, and I walked the column of 900 men checking on them.

I walked with the chaplain because I was his bodyguard. The Marine Corps doesn't have chaplains of their own. The Navy provides them, and their assistants, to the Marine Corps. They hate to admit it, but the Marine Corps is a department of the Navy. Marine Corps Order and secnav instruction forbid chaplains from carrying weapons, but they still need protection in combat. That was my job. I protected the chaplain. I went where he went, always on the alert for any threat to him, the Marines, or myself while helping him care for our Marines whether in a combat zone or back home. And so, I walked the line of resting Marines protecting the chaplain because we trained like we fought and fought like we trained, and I chatted with my friends in the battalion's rifle companies.

The Navy Corpsmen did the same, only they were checking Marines' feet for blisters. A Marine with bad feet is a waste of resources. In a rifle battalion, every Marine is important. A Marine and his weapon add to the firepower of the unit and aid in the mission of the infantry: to locate, close with, and destroy the enemy by fire and maneuver or repel his assault by fire and close combat. The religious ministry team and medical department exist to keep Marines healthy and well-adjusted so they can kill America's enemies with precision and without mercy. We all did our jobs well.

After walking up and down more mountains and another break at mile 10 of our hike, we received orders. Our battalion would execute a contact patrol to a location six miles distant. On a normal hike, we could zone out. One foot in front of the other until the pain, and the hike, ended. On a contact patrol, though, we aren't marching in a column; we are in combat formations, being tactical, alert, and moving quick. It isn't fun for anyone when you have a seventy-pound pack on your back. It's even less fun when you have a seventy-pound pack on your back and you weigh 120 pounds like me.

When the hike ended, our battalion commander, Lieutenant Colonel Glynn, and our Sergeant Major, Sergeant Major Ellis, told us that our strength, our professionalism, our military prowess, and the bond we shared as warriors made us the best warfighters in the world. Lieutenant Colonel Glynn and Sergeant Major said they were proud of us and proud to serve alongside us. I felt homesick, and I hadn't even left.

After they dismissed us, Lieutenant Colonel Glynn and Sergeant Major Ellis said I looked miserable. They told me that I looked like

I would not miss being in the grunts, which was funny. I was only there because they wouldn't let me leave. Refused to give me my checkout sheet until I did this one last thing with them because I belonged to them. And Marines only did stuff like that if they recognized you as one of their own. Once, years after that hike, I told General Glynn about that moment and how much I missed the Marines, that he had misjudged me. I don't think he remembered that hike or his speech.

Anyway. I had orders. To headquarters. I left my battalion and my Marines. I went home to take my boots off. No blisters, no hot spots. My feet were the only part of me that didn't hurt, thanks to my broken-in molded-to-my-feet boots.

I was wearing those boots a year later when I learned that Sergeant Major Ellis and Sergeant Ahlquist were killed (they were two of many KIA that pump). They were Magnificent Bastards, Marines of Second Battalion, Fourth Marines—my battalion. Sergeant Ahlquist, whom we called Rookie, was in Fox company. Sergeant Major Ellis selected him to be our Battalion Color Sergeant.

Rookie was killed on a foot patrol on 20 February 2007, in Ar Ramadi, Iraq. It was his second time in Ramadi. Staff Sergeant Williamson, Scottie, his platoon sergeant, told me Ahlquist's boot hit a dude name Knott in the back of the head when Rookie stepped on a double-stacked antitank mine. I think I remember reading in the CASREP: service member ID'd by tag in boot.

The night after Ahlquist was killed, his old platoon sergeant Gunny Shelton, called me. Crying. He failed his Marine, he said, because he transferred to a training unit. Rookie had come through one of Gunny's classes. Gunny believed he could and should have trained Ahlquist better. Prepared him for the dangers of Ramadi, he said. Taught him to survive, he said. Should have been there, he said.

Gunny called me because our five-year-old sons were friends and in the same kindergarten class. Because we deployed together. Because we were both Bastards. Because I was an RP. Because he should have been there. And because we both sat home in safety while our Marines went back to Iraq. I listened while he wept. I didn't say anything. It isn't like the movies. There are no words of comfort in those situations.

Sergeant Major Ellis was killed on 07 Feb 2007, in Barwanah, Iraq. I should have been there the day he died. But I had been transferred to that headquarters unit. Because I asked for it. Because I thought I wanted to be a civilian. I was in a parade for another Sergeant Major, safe in America, missing being in the grunts when I learned that Sergeant Major Ellis died. Marines, the other Sergeant Major said. I uh, I just got some bad news. Secure these Marines from this parade, he said. I have to go the White House. We called Division HQ the White House because it was a big white house.

I wasn't a boot. Hadn't been for a long time by then. My boots looked like infantry boots. Dog tag in the left boot, sweat- and salt-stained. Cracked. The suede wearing off. The treads worn down. I knew something bad had happened. I went to my office to check the CAS-REPS again.

7 February 2007, Sergeant Major Joseph J. Ellis, KIA Barwanah, Iraq. Family pending notification, the CASREP said. He was the only Marine Sergeant Major killed in our war. The last Marine Sergeant Major to get killed was Sergeant Major Big John Malnar. Big John was a 2/4 Magnificent Bastard. He was killed in Vietnam. Sergeant Major Ellis often referenced Big John. Idolized him. Emulated him, I think.

Sergeant Major Ellis and I deployed to Oki together in 2005. One time, at 0400, I went for a run. Sergeant Major Ellis and I met on the pathway. He had risen earlier than me.

RP, he said, what are you doing out here this early? Good morning, Sergeant Major, I said. I just want to get in a run and take it all in. We both stopped running. We looked, together, at the contours of Camp Hansen.

Take what in, he said. I think he was testing me, waiting to see if I would give the right answer, understood my place in our world. All of it, I said. This is Okinawa. Sixty years ago. Men our age. In our same companies fought, sometimes to the last man, here. I stopped talking. Yeah, it's heavy, he said after a long pause. A huge legacy to live up to, he said. He looked across the ground into the distance with those blue eyes of his. A lot of tradition, he said. Sometimes I wonder if he knew what would happen. They say guys like us know when their time is up, their luck run out.

The last time I saw Sergeant Major Ellis was in June of 2006, right after I had gotten promoted to First Class Petty Officer. I drove forty minutes from HQ to see him. Sergeant Major, I said, I picked up First. You don't pick up rank RP, he said. The dip in his mouth pushed out his lower lip. You pick up trash, he said. He grabbed a paper towel–lined foam cup from his desk, spit in it. You earn rank, he said. Is that rank trash or did you earn it, he said. He stared at me a moment, his blue eyes scrutinizing my bearing, searching for some form of weakness or fear to exploit. I earned it, Sergeant Major, I said, returning his stare. He glowered at me a moment longer. And then his face softened into an almost smile. Congratulations RP, it looks good on you, he said. He shook my hand. Now get the fuck out of my office, he said. Aye, Sergeant Major, I said. I left and never saw him again.

The CASREP said he died from exsanguination, which is the nice and clean way of saying he bled out after putting himself between a suicide bomber and the Marines he led. He bled to death so that his Marines could live. No one was there to hear me weep.

Sergeant Major Ellis wasn't my first, though. Gunny Menusa in 2003 was. Gunny Menusa was from First Combat Engineer Battalion. First CEB was my first battalion. You always remember your first. He and I had sons the same age. The last time I saw him was in Kuwait in a tent where we were having religious services. Gunny Menusa was worshipping Jesus with his eyes closed and hands raised. This was right after Staff Sergeant Davis showed me how to stab a man in the kidneys from behind to make him scream and scare the enemy on post or how to slice a man's throat or puncture his lungs in silence.

Sergeant Duane Rios from Bravo got killed after Gunny Menusa. Sergeant Rios had been in Charlie and all the guys in Charlie knew him but right before the war he got sent to Bravo because that's where the Marine Corps needed him. And when Whiskey got killed, I remember his wife crying at his funeral. And when HN Burnett got killed, I felt awful because I was there when the Hate Tank guys— Navy Corpsmen who ran Division Training, all combat vets—told Burnett that he was such a bad Corpsman that he would get himself or his Marines killed. All these years later I can hear his kid brother sobbing and saying no under the awning at his graveside service in Riverside National Cemetery. How hot it was in Navy Dress Blues that day and all of us taking our ribbons and FMF pins and throwing them as tribute, as a sign of respect, into the hole the size of his grave marker—there wasn't a casket. A few years after that I met his platoon leader after Catholic church services at the US Naval Academy chapel, my last duty station, as far from the battlefield as I could get, and the LT said Burnett was an amazing Corpsman. We had done our job, Burnett brought honor to himself to the Corpsman legacy. At least there was that.

But I didn't cry for any of those guys. And those aren't the only guys that I know who died, just some. But I don't want to list all the dead guys I know—knew—because that is just depressing. It's weird though, being young and knowing so many people in the past tense or knowing their memory as if they were still alive and keeping them alive by talking about them. Even now, all these years later, I still can't wrap my head around it. I accept it. It just is. But I don't know how to explain that. I was in a workshop once and the professor asked why I kept writing about this stuff, why didn't I just write one long essay and be done with it. I got angry, though I kept it all in. I got resentful. How could she or anyone in my class understand what I had just written? How could she ask why I didn't just write this and move on. Did any of them know what it was like to have a voice, a smile, a human violently taken years before anyone thinks they should? Did she know what it was like to live and still hear the voices of these men, smell their sweat, and sense the love in a smart-ass comment or even a sharp rebuke, to feel the sand, the mud, the . . . the everything of it and miss it?

So even though Sergeant Major Ellis wasn't my first, I cried. I cried because I remember having coffee with him every morning in my office and his froufrou hazelnut creamer and him walking with a Filipino kid on deployment and being so gentle with that child and him allowing my young son to swing on his arms before we deployed and that ridiculous high and tight of his and how he called me a good piece of gear and how I was so proud of being called a good piece of gear and I cried because I should have been there.

But I wasn't there. I was stateside because I wanted to get out, because my wife couldn't handle the pressure of the life. And I had agreed. And then when I changed my mind, when I realized that this life, as hard as it was, I wanted to go back, I got promoted and sent to a desk. To manage religious ministry teams like the ones I used to be in, to monitor training requirements and write evaluations. And go to staff meetings. I hated staff meetings. Still do.

At one staff meeting, the assistant Division chaplain made a joke about a Marine who'd just been killed. The chaplain said he thanked God for the dog tag in the boot because this Sergeant Parker had gotten blown to smithereens and that's how they ID'd him, he said. Then he chuckled. The rage I felt in that moment. The disrespect to one of our dead by this nondeploying outsider. You know, I said, trying to keep my rage in check but wanting him to know and hear he crossed a line. Not all of us are boots to the Division like you, sir. Some of us have been here awhile, I said. And some of us have friends that are dying while we sit here in stupid meetings listening to stupid officers say stupid things, I said. So maybe, just maybe, chaplain, sir. You should watch what you say. I got up and left the staff meeting. Sergeant Parker had come to 1st CEB as a boot when I was there. I had known him. And I had just found out about him a few moments before the chaplain opened his mouth.

We didn't use combat boots just to ID us. We used combat boots to memorialize a fallen brother.

The memorial: a pair of boots laced with a dog tag in them placed in front of an inverted rifle, with a Kevlar helmet on the butt stock and a pair of dog tags hanging from the magazine well. Some Marines walk to the rifle and boots that represented a Marine they knew, kneel or stand, and touch the dog tags of the fallen brother. Others salute. Some cry.

I have knelt, stood, cried, and saluted at more of those memorials than I care to think about.

Anyway. I've been out a while now. I figured my feet needed a rest after all the marching, and running, and humping and fighting and dying. Nowadays, I wear Vans, sometimes Chuck Taylors, usually dress shoes. The hardest thing I do is miss the old days. The farthest I have to walk is maybe 200 yards to get food, ironic since I learned to shoot that far and there isn't anything on my back when I do walk. The risk to any people I know dying is pretty low, no one is trying to kill me, and I don't have to prepare to kill or be killed.

I still have those combat boots. I keep them in my footlocker, where I keep old uniforms and mementos from Iraq. My dog tag is still laced into my left boot. They are encrusted with Iraqi and Kuwaiti sand and Okinawan clay and Camp Pendleton dirt. The laces are stiff. The treads are almost bare. The suede is almost completely rubbed off. But my feet remember them, and when I put them on they fit like I never took them off.

THROWBACK
THURSDAY

One of the TAs is listening to Jimmy Eat World's "In the Middle,"
and then it's Spring Break '03 and I'm on the *Bonhomme Richard* in
the middle of the Gulf or Indian or Pacific Ocean, only I'm not. It's a
Thursday and I'm sitting at a desk in an office at the university where
I teach and it's 2017. But I swear I'm on that ship.

I can smell Charlie Pugh's feet that reek so bad it makes us wanna
retch every time he takes his boots off and we all yell at him to put
his boots on and he says sorry and I can hear Delphia strumming
his guitar and singing "Fuzzy Woman Whose Bush Looked Like It
Was from the '70s," a song he wrote, and he is leaning up against
his coffin rack where Charlie Pugh is putting his boots back on so
we don't get sick and I can see and hear big Jay Bennington walking
through berthing looking for Rosas, who probably fucked something
up again, and Bear is sitting in his chair in his darkened row of coffin racks across from mine practicing singing "Remix to Ignition"
and Davis is drenched in sweat from doing rack hops because Bear
said so and Ryan McDaniel tells me he plays the drums and listens
to Jimmy Eat World and Pallan and Banshee are sitting in a corner
by their racks talking about their band and we all have cammies on

and I can smell the diesel fuel on them because it's in the water and the stench of feet that have been in boots too long and in my office at the university where I teach my stomach turns a little and my blood pressure rises and I can hear the turning of the ship's machinery and I start to sweat.

All the while, I can hear the TAs across the lab chat and laugh and listen to Jimmy Eat World and I realize they were young teens or even children then and now young adults, in their early 30s even and I am in my 40s and even though it's 2017 all those sights and sounds and smells and memories are as fresh as when they happened and the machinery I hear is the building's AC unit but isn't it weird that a song can do that?

Isn't it weird that I can be in two places at once though I'm not?

That's how it happens, you know. It isn't ever just war things: explosions or pot shots and gun fights or blood and death. Sometimes it's the overlooked things, the things outsiders don't know about because they don't ever ask and we don't ever tell. And that's why we get so weird sometimes because it happens in the most random of ways at the most random of times. And what's weirder is that though my stomach turned and my blood pressure rose and I started to sweat, and even though Pugh's feet were godawful and Delphia's voice cracked a little when he sang, I miss those guys and those things.

THE BEST MEAL
I EVER HAD

....

The best meal I ever had was Spam and rice in Iraq for Spring Break '03. We were in the middle of a severe turab windstorm. Everyone thinks it was a shamal, but shamal means north in Arabic and this storm came from the south. Doc Pete Kamau had an ear infection, and his ear was so swollen that it was twice the size of a normal ear and puffy, so puffy we thought it might burst, but there wasn't anything we could do so he sat and suffered in silence. Later he and Doc San would find blankets and get scabies from them, but that was a few weeks away.

Anyway, the windstorm was so bad that it shut down everything. No logistics, no operations, no nothing. Just howling wind and sand, and grit, and wind. And the BAS tent. We hadn't eaten anything in days because you couldn't open your canteens to fill the MRE heater because the water would turn to mud from the grit and the sand would fill an open MRE pouch in seconds and no one wanted to eat spoonfuls of sand. We were sick of MREs anyway.

I've got just the thing for a day like today, Doc Molinos, a Filipino Guamanian, not a Chamorro, said during a brief lull in wind velocity.

He broke out the sterilizer and a rice cooker and a can of Spam. I don't remember anything about him cooking it, I just remember him spooning some rice and a perfectly cooked piece of Spam into my dirty canteen cup. I didn't even bother cleaning it because what was the point? The wind was still blowing, and dust and grit were swirling in the air. But it was warm food. And for just a few minutes, we forgot that we hadn't had real food or showered or changed socks or slept (well) or couldn't breathe and couldn't keep the dust from coating our eyelashes and the corners of our mouths or the creases in our skin in days.

Or maybe it was the time when we rolled up on some Iraqi training camp and had stew. Before we got there, 3/7 killed everything that moved. Marines do that. Anyway, the only thing they hadn't killed were these pigeons that the dead base commander was raising and, well, he was dead. And we were hungry. We were down to one meal a day and my last MRE was a beef patty with wheat snack bread and cheese spread—MRE nomenclature for cheeseburger—that came with a strawberry shake. The shakes were legendary. I had found one. Those were MRE gold. But I didn't want an MRE milk shake or beef patty with wheat snack bread and cheddar cheese spread. So there we were with one MRE a day and still no showers or clean clothes or sleep and these live pigeons.

Doc San, who would later get scabies with Pete Kamau and then even later get busted for trying to (allegedly) sell gear on eBay, went foraging with Doc DeRosales, the Filipino doc who'd go on to lose a toe or two—I forget how many—on the next deployment, the same deployment when my brother would puncture a lung. I went foraging on my own. Not my best decision. You aren't supposed to go off alone in a war zone. That's how you get taken or dead or both. The docs found a big sack of rice and some carrots and onions and potatoes. A whole shit ton, they said. I found a busted water pipe that had water still pouring out of it. I also found a propane tank and a stove in some trash-ridden hallway that smelled like dead guy. I grabbed the stove and asked Doc Moose to grab the propane tank because it was really fucking heavy and I couldn't carry my weapon

and the stove and the propane tank. And Doc Moose was like 6'6"
and 200 something pounds and lifted the propane tank like it was
a small child and we carried the stuff to the ambulance and then we
remembered that those pigeons were in the coop over where I found
the busted pipe that would become the shower. So Doc San and Doc
DeRosales went and grabbed a couple because what did the dead guy
need them for and made a stew.

The whole company and the battalion headquarters could smell the
stew and they came in a line with their empty canteen cups and cut-
in-half MRE bags for bowls and the docs filled the bowls and our XO
who was acting CO said do I want to know where you got this RP
and I said no. And then he said we weren't supposed to be taking
from the people here and will there be breakfast and the docs said
yes and there was and we got to shower and have a sort of real meal.
Twice in a twelve-hour period. That was more real food and more
showers than we'd had in weeks.

The Iraqi bread was pretty good, too. So good that we got ordered
to convoy out to the ville and get some from the local baker. We had
to set security and the people were acting suspicious and that was
where I almost shot some kid in the face and had to rescue Doc
DeRosales, who would later get his toe(s?) blown off from a crowd
because they wouldn't leave him alone. All for some bread. But it was
real good bread. Better when it was warm.

Right before the whole First Marine Division got the shits at our
camp at Ad Diwaniyah, after we were told we were going home, after
the country was supposedly secured, we had tray-rat breakfast and
Iraqi Cokes. This is after I ate the pigeons, by the way, which makes
what happens next so funny. Since we weren't fighting and moving
and were preparing to go home, we could get supplies and mail
again. We had green eggs and some kind of sausage. They served
it out of those green mermite food cans. I don't know why the eggs
were green. I know they were powdered and tasted weird, but there
weren't a lot of options. And we hadn't had the green eggs since leaving Kuwait. And we had Cokes. Everyone got at least one.

And then we got the shits. Viral gastroenteritis. The entire First
Marine Division. I don't know if it was the Cokes, since they
used local water, or the green eggs or the chemicals used to treat
our drinking water or the local dates that seemed to appear from
nowhere or the local food we'd scavenged or what. I just know we all
got it. Every one of the several thousand Marines and sailors of First
Marine Division.

When I told the story about the pigeon stew to my now ex-wife and
civilian friends from before the war, they all looked at me in disgust
because I ate pigeons and stole a stove and food, and I didn't understand why they couldn't see the beauty of that meal.

And even when a friend asked me what the best meal I had ever had
was and I told her all these stories, she looked at me and asked if it
was the meals that were so good or the circumstances that made the
meals so good.

I answered yes.

THANK YOU FOR YOUR SERVICE

WE REPRESENT THE VA, the man in the buy-two-get-one-free suit says. I never served but I want to say thank you for your service, he says. For your sacrifice, he says. I watch him. I only hear the never served part. The woman, blonde, West Virginian, speaks next. I just want to say that I never served either, but it's my duty and honor to take care of you, she says. At the VA we are honored to serve you. We understand what you've been through and we want to help, we'll answer your questions and tell you what benefits are available to you as veterans, they say.

Did you file your claim yet, one fat Navy chief whispers to another as the VA reps end the brief and give us a five-minute break. No, the other says. Well, you need to get that one hundred percent, the fat one says and laughs. Got my hearing test done, he says, told the doc I can't hear shit and my knees and my back. Damn Boats, the other says. Give me my hundred percent and my retirement pay and I'll be set. Twenty years on the boat, I've earned it, the fat one says. The other chief laughs. The fat one laughs. I hear you, the other one says. I say nothing. We are in civilian clothes. No ranks today, just names. And what about the poor bastard who only did four years and got blown the fuck up or shot up or watched his buddy die, does he deserve it less? Does he have to wait behind you for treatment at the clinic when we get out, if he even asks for help, which he won't? I bet you'll love it when people say thank you for service won't you. It was an honor, you'll say. It was so hard, you'll say. When the fuck ever was it hard for you? He's right, some other chief says. You're an ass, this chief says to the fat one. I didn't think I'd said that out loud.

MY WIFE, LISA, DOESN'T SLEEP MUCH. Takes or has taken Lunesta, Ambien, some other chemical with bad side effects but should let you sleep, and it affects her bad but doesn't let her sleep. She tosses. Turns. Gets up. Lies down. In my sleep, I hear her. She whimpers when she does sleep. Shakes. Fights. Dives for cover. No, I didn't, or none of that happened, or so do you sometimes, she says in the morning. Or in the afternoon. Or anytime I bring it up. It did, I say. No, it didn't, she says. Sometimes she says sorry for waking me.

One day at breakfast at the VFW hall, she tells me that that man over there is her old Sergeant Major. This one time before Holly got killed, she says, we were on our way to breakfast at the chow hall on Blue Diamond when a rocket came in and he dove on me and threw us in a ditch. The rocket exploded where I had been walking, she says. She shrugs. When Holly died, he took it real hard, she says. She worked directly for him, she says. Lisa touches the black bracelet on her wrist etched with Holly's name and date. I already know that she helped pack Holly's things to send them home.

After years of convincing, she applies for VA disability. Combat-related PTSD. She was in imminent danger, someone she cared about died, she was in country for a year. Requirements met. It's just depression, the VA says. No, we didn't look at the evidence, the VA says.

When we go places, to Veterans Day things, to Memorial Day things, the older vets and civilians come up, shake my hand, tell Lisa how proud of me she must be. They thank her for supporting her veteran. We laugh, Lisa and I. She's a vet, too, I say. Did a year in Ramadi when it was the Wild West and dudes were dying fast and messy, I say. Oh, they say. Confused. They walk away. Forget to thank her for her service.

WALKING OUR DOG WE SEE HIM. White male, mid-twenties, just overweight, full beard. A contractor ball cap and paracord bracelet. A limp. Did you serve, I say. Yeah, he says. Is that where you got the limp, we say. Yeah, on an op, he says. Have you gotten the VA to look at it, Lisa says. No, I want to go Special Forces and I figure it will ruin my chances if I have a bad knee, he says. So you know, I'm trying to keep it out of my file, he says. I nod. So you were Army, I say. Navy, he says. Oh, us too, we say. What was your rate, we say. I was PSD, he says. But what did you do in the Navy, I say. I guarded high-profile individuals on convoys in Iraq, he says. It was classified, he says. I was in Iraq, First Marine Division, I know what PSD is, I say. What was your rate, I say. Navy jobs are called rates. I was a medic, he says. The Navy doesn't have medics, we say. Navy Corpsmen would never call themselves medics unless maybe they were talking to an outsider. We weren't outsiders. I look at Lisa, she looks at me. She shakes her head no. Well, good luck with everything, we say. We walk on. Fuck that guy, we say.

A week later that same man with the beard and the hat and the limp and the paracord bracelet is in line to claim his free Veterans Day veteran's appreciation meal at Golden Corral. I want to beat his ass, throw him out of line, ask him for his ID or DD214. He doesn't have to provide one.

People thank him for his service.

ON A FRIDAY MORNING, Veterans Day as a matter of fact, the graduate student sees me. I am hungover after celebrating the Marine Corps Birthday with my son and another Marine and my wife and am getting ready to sit on a panel discussion about self-care with my colleagues. We are there to talk about rest and refitting. I am there to talk because the best thing I can think of to celebrate Veterans Day is to serve my community of writers and students.

The graduate student who sees me, Summer, is a panel host. She walks up to me. Michael, she says. I have been thinking about you because today, she says. She begins to stammer. I don't know if it's okay, or how you prefer or if you prefer—she stops, looks at me. I look at her. The room fills with students and community members.

You can thank me for my service if you want to or if it feels right, I say. She smiles. Thanks me for my service. You mean so much to us, she says. I wanted to honor you in a way that feels right to you, she says.

I smile back. It was an honor to serve, I say. I was glad to do it, I say. And I would do it again. Thank you, I say to her. For taking time and listening to me and getting to know me.

....

WHAT IT'S LIKE TO COME HOME

....

Billy Pilgrim became unstuck in time. Norman Bowker drove around a lake in circles. Nick Adams went fishing. They did these things, not because they went to war, but because they came home. They came home and everyone said they wanted to know what the war was like, only everyone didn't. People wanted to be told the war was wrong or heroic. People wanted to tell Billy and Nick and Norman how wrong or heroic the war was. People wanted the kill stories, the trauma stories, what they'd read about or seen on TV or in movies. They wanted to know how scared Billy and Nick and Norman were because the people who asked would be scared and they wanted reassurances. Reassurances that the askers were not cowards. Reassurances that the askers were right not to enlist or fight. Reassurances that the askers were just as good as them. Reassurances that the askers had nothing to prove, though they clearly have something to prove. Billy and Nick and Norman probably thought about home on the way home and how great it would be. Because how could it not be? It wasn't there after all. Then they got home and realized home wasn't what they remembered.

Because coming home is biting into a warm, soft, chocolate chip cookie but realizing too late it's oatmeal raisin. A bait and switch.

Or maybe it's like drinking one of those La Croix drinks where the can says cherry and you're thirsty so you take a big drink, but it tastes like bad seltzer water and the distorted, broken memory of what cherry should taste like. All expectation and no delivery.

Or maybe coming home is like a surprise party only you hate surprises because you don't like loud noises or people jumping out and shouting at you when you walk into a darkened room and never have.

Coming home is waiting for the pleasure of cool, soft carpet between your toes, the smell of Suavitel and your son's skin, being excited to be away from the noise and smell of the guys, of ship, of war, the peace of taking a shit or a shower alone without ten other guys doing the same thing at the same time all yelling while doing it, and dreaming of sitting on your old couch or chair—you know the one, the one that's soft and broken in, molded to your body like your combat boots are molded to your feet—and watching TV or sitting in silence, anticipating the drive home on I-5, windows down with no gear or weapons handy, only your wife's hand and the smell of anise and the Pacific Ocean's salt, wondering what the reunion will be like, what you'll say to her, what she'll look like, only to remember that your wife sent you a letter a couple of months ago that you guys had moved, and the void in your memory because you don't know where you live and can't drive there and you don't know what the new house looks like or smells like causes a weird surge of feeling—you later learn it's called anxiety—then another surge from getting to the new place in the passenger seat and not recognizing any of the furniture because your wife thought she should get new stuff, and sex not lasting nearly as long as you'd hoped and sleeping in the quiet only to wake because it was quiet, too quiet, and you don't know where you are.

Coming home is remembering how proud of you people were when you left and not being able to wait to see them, but then when you are home those people seem to have forgotten that you were gone at all. And when you rush home to meet them you don't want to say, hey guys, I'm home from war or I wore this uniform because you thought war vets did that when they came home, and people ask you why you are so dressed up and where have you been and say things like you look like you've lost weight, you look tired, and then folks realize you just came back from a war deployment and oh my gosh, it's so great to see you and let's go to lunch, so they take you to lunch at Johnny Carino's, only it's loud in the restaurant or maybe it isn't, but it's just loud to you because you can hear the conversations of every single person in the section of your restaurant who aren't at your table, and every clink of silverware on plate and dull thud of a glass or bottle being placed on the table after someone drinks, and every mint being unwrapped when people pay their bill, and you can smell all of the perfumes and colognes that people are wearing and how all of a sudden the room is closing in on you and you are hot and you don't know what to order because there are so many choices and you can't drown out the noise of everything, and why are you paying attention to everything all while not paying attention to anything anyone at the table is saying because you'd rather be with your buddies or somewhere quiet with less people and you wonder what they are doing and if they are enjoying being home, and then someone at the table says something else and your wife nudges you to get your attention because honey so-and-so is talking to you and the person says thank you for going over there and fighting for us and you're a hero, and it surprises you because you were pretty sure that people only said that in the movies and you say, oh, uh, you're welcome, but I'm not a hero and you feel awkward because why are you a hero and what are they thanking you for when an hour ago they had forgotten you had even left. And then someone else at the table asks you if you missed your friends, meaning them, the ones from your old life before the war, and you don't want to say no but saying yes would be a lie, so you just kind of hedge and say, oh, well, you know there isn't time to think about home and whatnot because you have to stay focused on the job, which of course leads to the questions what job, what was it like, and how do you explain seeing oil running everywhere and collateral damage and dead people and displaced people, that you are capable of causing great harm, and what protecting a chaplain actually means, and what it feels like to hear that someone you know got killed in a gunfight on a Sunday afternoon at a Johnny Carino's. How do you explain that you never thought once about these people and now you regret coming home to see them and you can't wait to get back in the car and get home to Camp Pendleton, and they just keeping talking platitudes and things they think they are supposed to say and you get angry because they persist and won't stop talking—why do civilians never shut up?—and you get a little resentful and you say look, I'm not trying to be rude, but I didn't think about any of you. All of this America and apple pie stuff isn't real, I really only thought about not dying, my friends not dying, not getting my chaplain or my Marines killed, and not doing anything that would dishonor me or my Marines or my son. I'm sorry, but you just weren't that important at the time, and the table goes quiet, in fact, every person in the restaurant was silent because you are a little louder and more forceful than you or anybody remembers, and then there is that brief, awkward pause before everything goes back to normal.

Or maybe coming home is a lot like being Rip Van Winkle. You leave and you're gone, then you come back and you feel the same while everyone else stayed behind so you think they should be the same. Only no one is. You are older, you feel older, tired, but you were gone and you don't think you or anyone has changed, so you aren't prepared for how different everyone at home is, how their lives don't involve or include you, your brain can't process that time didn't slow down, that people and things aren't how you left them, how you imagined them, and how you wanted them to be when you came home. And also, you aren't the same even though you don't feel different and the people you are sort of mad at for changing, like, let's say, your wife, won't stop telling you how different you are and she doesn't even know you anymore and she misses who you used to be and she may as well be speaking a foreign language because you have no idea what she means.

But you don't smile much anymore, and one of your seniors who comes to see you says he is worried about you because your smile is gone and you are so quiet now. So quiet that even you notice and

WHAT IT'S LIKE TO COME HOME

every once in a while you go off on your own and stare at the ocean or play guitar alone for hours in your garage and most everyone outside the military you talk to either doesn't care and isn't interested or is an expert and wants to tell you how wrong or heroic you were. And all you really want is someone to listen as you try to understand the waste of war and the hardship and the aliveness of war and not getting killed, but you also really just want to be left alone, so you kind of wish you had a lake to drive around or a river to fish. And you are unstuck in time—being home and in Iraq in the present at once—and that is just the way it is now. You recognize it and you don't fight it anymore. And eventually you get so used to being in the past and the present at the same time that it doesn't even bother you that much anymore.

Coming home is boring. And not that you are an adrenaline junkie or anything. But no one moves with a purpose or seems to care about anything except things that don't matter in the grand scheme of things. You go from work or school to home and home to work and you zone out while doing it and you zone out when your neighbor talks about splitting the cost of good grass for your yards, for example, because you don't have to look out for IEDs or dudes hiding RPGs or AKs or dudes on cellphones checking out your positions to call mortars in on you. No one is going to try and kill you (probably) and you don't miss that, but you do kinda miss it and you kinda wish a motherfucker would but they won't.

Coming home is like being told you are broken and unreadable over the radio. What you say isn't being received, can't be maybe, on the other end. You aren't sure if it's them or you, so you move to a different position, check the handset, the battery, the antenna, and send it again, trying to be understood, but the people you're communicating with still can't read you. Only instead of hearing static they hear anger in anything and everything you say. Which confuses you because you aren't angry. Okay, maybe you are a little angry at being misunderstood or judged, or maybe not angry just frustrated, but don't you have a right to be? And you wonder if maybe they are afraid of you and that's why they see anger, or maybe you're too direct and don't let things slide but you don't know how to be anything else, and still you try to get a signal out and it still comes back broken and unreadable, so eventually you just stop trying.

Coming home is walking in the dark. But instead of fumbling around in the dark and stubbing your toe your eyes adjust. Okay, at first there is a lot of stumbling because your eyes haven't adjusted and there is a lot of stubbing toes and a lot, A LOT, of cussing, but you just keep walking and walking and walking because what the hell else are you going to do. And then one day as you keep walking in the dark, you realize that none of your now friends are in danger of dying and neither are you. That you have friends now, not just civilians you interact with. That you get showers and food. That you have a job that you enjoy and you have people who make work fun and you get to see your kids grow up and get married, and then you realize that maybe you aren't actually in the dark anymore.

Or maybe, you were in the dark and coming home was like walking through a tunnel and after you come to the end and back into the light, you might still need a lake to drive around or a river to fish, and you will probably always be unstuck in time. But you are okay with it.

Because you came home when they didn't. And you can live with that.

WHAT THE WORKSHOP DID

On a clear Saturday in July of 2016, or maybe it might have been 2017, we file into the room at the Cam. The big one with all the windows, and without a word each of us sits facing the door and all the windows. It's me and my wife, Lisa, both of us Iraq vets, and Jose and his wife, Kaci, and Ray—whom we call Chief—and his wife, Jose and Chief are Afghanistan vets, and then two Vietnam vets sit next to them in that order.

We get there fifteen minutes prior because we get everywhere fifteen minutes prior because fifteen minutes prior means you're on time. And since we are there fifteen minutes prior to the start of the writer's workshop for civilians and war vets, we watch the hippie protesters amble in. No, really. Hippie protesters. One of my classmates from graduate school organized this event to help bridge the gap between us vets and civilians. It just so happens that the civilians who show up were hippie protesters during the Vietnam War. That's what they told us later, anyway. The Vietnam vets and the hippie protesters recognize one another. They don't know each other, they just recognize which group the other belongs to. Without introduction, on instinct. Another female vet shows up, too, and she sits in the middle between us vets and the hippie protesters.

We get started and the workshop leader says he is a Vietnam vet and was a Marine during Vietnam. Was not is. Marines are present tense, not past. This gets Jose and Chief's attention, they are Marines, and mine and Lisa's, too, because we were Greenside Navy RPs assigned to Marines. The Vietnam vets, both Army, were interested because they fought over the same ground as this guy. Family. Except I am sitting closest to him and he doesn't feel right. I don't mean like something visible. Or that he did anything wrong. He just didn't feel right. As in I didn't feel like I was home next to him like I do with Jose or Chief or any other Marine that I've met. That sense of familiarity and quiet confidence—not that Marines are quiet so much— the feeling in the blood and bone of kinship. It's like what I said earlier about instinct. I don't know if that makes any sense to anyone who has never felt that.

So he does his writing workshop thing and we do the writing workshop thing and then a professor from the university—my colleague—gives a presentation on martial music from the Civil War era and tells us that the veteran and civilian divide started during the Civil War when northerners with money could buy their way out of service. And the North was far from battle (except for Pennsylvania and Maryland) and the South was the battleground, but that tiny bit of removal from the war for the northerners opened a chasm between those who experienced the war and those who only heard or read about it. I didn't know that, but it makes sense.

After that, the past-tense Marine starts talking about folk music in Vietnam and how powerful and true it was. He says that the music made him ashamed to be in Vietnam doing the things he did— though he never really said what he did or maybe I just don't remember. Then he says he was ashamed to be a Marine. The hippie protesters all kind of nod and murmur their understanding. It reminds me of church, the way the used-to-be hippie protesters reacted. Like when someone gives a testimony and people murmur amen, that kind of feeling.

The past-tense Marine looks at us on the vet side of the room. We are silent. We look back at him. We on the Marine side of the house had never heard anything like this before and the two Army Vietnam vets knew that Marines were never ashamed of being Marines.

Nothing really came of it. Nothing other than him pausing a little and looking at us waiting for us to approve or absolve him, which we didn't. I knew he didn't feel right. I kind of pitied him a little. Then I forgot about him. He was one of them, not us. The hippies, I mean. And he was one of those vets. The broken ones who are so ashamed. The make-us-roll-our-eyes vets. Because most of us are doing okay and not ashamed and crippled by "what we've done." But almost no one is interested in those of us vets figuring it out and doing okay, which makes it funny(ier) that we are at a workshop to tell our stories to civilians, since odds are they want his story, the workshop leader's, the one they know and need to believe. Seems to me that vets like us in that room who saw some shit, survived some shit, and are struggling or have struggled but are figuring it out are too complicated to understand.

The looks and murmurs of the civilians are what I remember most about that moment. So . . . affirming. So . . . righteous. Like they expected past-tense Marine to say he was ashamed and embarrassed. I run into that a lot. The expectation and assumption that I am ashamed of my time with the Marines and in Iraq. As if being in a writing program and writing itself is some sort of penance. That I have seen the light and renounced my warlike ways. That I will use my words to make reparations or some shit. And when I don't, they can't wrap their head around it. Like why am I not a good liberal? Why don't I adopt their politics? What's wrong with me?

To be fair, the fake hero-worshipping crowd are the same way. They want to know why I am not a good Bible-thumping flag-waving conservative hero who hates them dirty Muslims or whatever. What do I mean I don't appreciate their politics? What's wrong with me?

It almost never occurs to anyone that we could be okay "with what we've done," whatever the fuck that means, or that we don't want their pity or adulation. It doesn't occur to them that our complicated existence threatens the safety of their made-up worldview, their illusion of peace and safety or righteous anger at the heathen. The fact that neither of those things are true—that the world isn't a safe place where evil is just a construct and we are just cogs in the racist, imperialist America and that we have a duty to kill the heathen in the name of white Jesus and America—are too difficult to accept, so instead people want our stories to fit into easy molds so they can continue living in their right(eous) lives. But I digress.

Before lunchtime we read some things we wrote or felt. I read an essay I wrote. The past tense Marine cautions me about being too passionate and one-dimensional, that I should talk about my (anti-war) feelings about the war more, that my writing could be construed as too prowar, though he did appreciate my work. I think it was weird he said the same thing the hippies and other outsiders tell me I should feel and write about. That there should be trauma and sorrow and repentance and not love or acceptance or acceptance and forward movement. But he was one of them, not us. I smile and say thank you because it is the polite thing to do. Others in the group decline to read.

Then past-tense Marine reads something he'd written about doing what he did in Vietnam for the citizens even though they never asked. He asks, in that piece, for approval or acknowledgment or something. Jose and Chief and Lisa and I look at each other. We never did anything for the people back home. That's true, by the way. Cliché or not. The guys on your left and right are the only ones who matter. Not wanting to let those guys down. That's why we do what we do. Not for the civilian back home who doesn't even have a clue that we are gone. Never. We learn real quick that thinking about the folks back home is a good way to get yourself or, worse, someone else messed up or dead.

The day progresses and when it comes time to share things about ourselves, I don't remember what the hippie protesters said, other than that they said they were hippie protesters. I do remember the past-tense Marine listening to us vets talk. Watching us. Leaning toward us. And then he began to feel right. And then out of nowhere after a hippie says something about not understanding our bonds as family, how she would be afraid to go to war and to kill and protect others, the past-tense Marine says that you don't think about your own fear, just the guys around you, that those bonds are unbreakable. And that even though he said those things earlier he still felt closer to us than them even though the hippies assumed he was one of them. Talk about surprises. He feels right after that. I wonder if he just needed to be reminded of who he was. Maybe he needed be around some of his folks.

I think that's true. That we get amnesia of sorts after the boom, after we come home, after the war. We are so used to being judged by everyone else for "what we've done" that we forget that we were warriors. Proud, noble, selfless, tired, scared, hungry, dirty, and part of a family. That perceptions of people who've never been to war, who judge us by their safe-at-home-in-America standards, who've never been as close to a human's original state as us, weigh us down. We start to think that we were wrong and we should be ashamed because everyone else says they would be and we should be, too. We stop exercising and breathing deep and enjoying the life that we fought to keep. We forget that no one is going to die if we don't get that TPS report in, and we get overwhelmed by bills and HOAs and all of it because we got to be freed from it in country. And then because somehow we still don't fit in, we check out early because we forget who we are—not were—and then civilians seem surprised to hear that vets kill themselves at the cyclic rate. Maybe a good dose of remembering who we are would help. Maybe listening to us and letting us tell the story as it is, and not as people want it to be, would keep us on this side of life. But I digress again.

Anyway, after the no longer a past-tense Marine drops his bombshell, the other female vet who sits in the middle of us and the protesters shares. Turns out she is a Marine. And when it came her time to share, she starts crying about feeling guilty for missing out on the war and sending her Marines off without her. I know what that's like, but to be honest, it strikes me as a little weird that she started crying because she said she was a Staff Sergeant. No Marine Staff Sergeant I ever knew or saw cried unless they'd lost a guy. Maybe. And even then. They never really bawled so much as shed some tears and sniffled. She. Is. Bawling. Needs fistfuls of Kleenex bawling. It seems off to me and Lisa, but in those situations where everyone is being open and honest you can't say things like, this seems off to me, that most every female Marine I ever knew was tough as any male Marine, and she was making those female Marines look bad. Not because she was crying. Not because she was a woman. But because it didn't seem genuine. It's hard to explain, and I don't want to cop out. But we live by our senses. And when our gut says something is wrong it is. I just need you to trust me on this.

I wish I could tell you that we all healed and had a better understanding of each other and sang some folk song together after we vets repented for whatever it is people always seem to want us to repent from and the bridge we feel between us was bridged. But that wouldn't be true.

The truth is I went home and started thinking about how way back in the caveman days, this would have ended differently. How we would have come back from a raid or a battle and told our stories to the folks who stayed behind. How it was understood and implied that we *did* do what we did for them, because our tribe's—those who fought and those who stayed behind—actual survival and freedom depended on it, that we defended ourselves from raiders or we raided and conquered someone else and took their supplies, and how we would be able to survive as a group a little longer. We would talk about the ones we lost in the fight, and together we and those who stayed behind would honor our dead as a group. And they would accept us—love us—as we were, for what and who we were. They would listen to our stories and welcome us home, not doubt our stories or try to make us and our stories fit into their worldview. I guess you could say those were simpler times, but we also had to worry a lot about getting schwacked by some other tribe or getting eaten by an animal or something, so there is that. But I still think it's true about the simpler times and unity and the power of shared proximity to death and danger.

And I thought a lot about what my colleague said about the veteran and civilian divide and how after the Vietnam warfighters were treated, we overcorrected, and so we have these type of workshops to bring us home or whatever, which aren't bad and I think they are a good idea and started with good intentions, but they never seem to be on our terms. It seems that we have these type of workshops not for us but for those who didn't go, which could be fine if those who didn't go accepted our stories as they are and not as they want or expect them to be. It can be frustrating. It can make you not want to talk or share.

And the truth is, I didn't go back for the second day of the thing. We almost did, Lisa and I. We even got to the parking lot, but Lisa and I argued because the events of the day before brought some stuff up that she hadn't counted on and she didn't know how to deal with. So she did what we all do. What we know how to do. She fought. She fought with me, and I fought right back. And then we left. To continue the fight. Lisa fought to express rage, grief, and pain, and I fought to get her to a place where she saw me as an ally, not an enemy. Neither of those things happened. Instead, we fought to exhaustion and then cried in each other's arms. Tired of the pain, tired of the misunderstanding, tired of the fighting, tired of no one listening.

Lisa's friend Holly was killed in that VBIED attack in Fallujah in '05. The one that killed or wounded eleven women Marines—some of whom were Lisa's roommates and friends—and some other folks. Lisa was supposed to be on that truck—read: would have been hurt or killed—but her chaplain pulled her off it before it left the wire, and Lisa was pissed off that he wouldn't let her go outside the wire to do her part, as she saw it. Holly died because she had taken out her SAPIs and opened her flak because Iraq is hot and Holly was hot and so when the VBIED detonated, she took a chunk of shrapnel in the chest.

Holly's anniversary was a few days after this writing workshop. And that crying female Marine Staff Sergeant who we learned not only didn't go but missed the war by two years but wanted in on the trauma hence all the crying and guilt and how the hippies fawned all over her because she had the story and tears that they and most other outsiders gravitate to made my wife angry, resentful, and unwilling to share her story because that other female vet's story was the one the group heard first and wanted to hear anyway. Lisa wanted none of it. Like most of us, she could hack it, did hack it, and didn't want pity.

I'd been in enough workshops that I wasn't surprised or even disappointed at how the first day turned out. I was prepared for it. Lisa wasn't. And she wasn't prepared for her story to come up and ambush her either. And that's something I wish people knew. That when someone asks us to tell our story and we decide to tell it, it costs us something to revisit those places, to resee those friends, and to rehear voices that were silenced. That when someone asks us to tell a story and we tell it, we made a risk-management decision. We decide (and hope) that the risk of being judged or misunderstood does not outweigh the benefits of (finally) being understood and heard.

Now that I think of it, after the past-tense Marine shared his Vietnam stories and shame, the other Vietnam vets clammed up. They talked to us vets during the breaks, but with other folks, little to nothing. They didn't share a lot during the discussions either and only answered questions they were asked, and they answered in as few words as possible. After seeing how the crowd reacted, how they accepted The Story, they probably didn't see the point in trying to tell their story. I can't say I blame them.

A LONG AND INCOMPLETE LIST OF SOME OF THE THINGS YOU CAN'T (DON'T) TALK ABOUT

1. The first time someone calls you killer you're a boot and haven't killed anyone yet and maybe you don't want to kill anyone at all because sure you joined thirteen days before 9/11 and after 9/11 you were ready to kill the people responsible for making the people you love cry and afraid but that was just talk but killer as a name as in someone who kills another person sounds wrong but then you hear it so much and they say it with such reverence that you don't hear it at all and you think of course you're a killer whatever else could you be until you get around real killers and you realize that you aren't and neither are they really but you're a boot and you don't know any better and they see in you that you can kill with and for them

and you would because you have seen pictures of their families and they have seen pictures of yours and you know their first names and things about them and they have come over to your house to grill or you have gone to theirs for the holidays and you love these guys and you'd be damned if someone tried to kill them and so they respect you and so you think yes you are a killer and people are no longer people unless they are people you know otherwise they are targets like at the rifle range and it takes only three pounds of pressure to kill a man and doesn't that sound psycho and yet you know that you wouldn't hurt anyone unless you had to even though you were ready to kill that one fat ten-year-old because he wouldn't stay back and you didn't even say I'll kill you or anything because that really only happens in the movies and you just chambered a round for him to see since you already had a round chambered and really only needed to squeeze the trigger and you remember it's only three pounds of pressure and as you bring your weapon up and he sees the barrel and he sees your eyes and he and the adults who are pressing in on you back up and you remember the Sapper Sergeant Bear who you call Bear or Mike saying that the moment when you look at another man over your weapon or he looks at you over yours and he sees in your eyes that you have the power to kill or let him live and in your soul he sees that you will kill him that you are god in that moment to that man and you are never the same after and you remember laughing a little to ease the tension of the moment but then you've become that man even though you are really just a kid in his mid-twenties with a son a few years younger than the kid you aim your weapon at and his eyes get big and the men's eyes in the crowd get big and they move back and they laugh then you laugh and then you realize how tense you are but how your heart isn't beating fast this time because you weren't scared only tired and your desire to get home to see your kid outweighed this kid's right to live but thank god he didn't want to die that day and you had already been shot at and you had already seen another man through the iron sights of your rifle and almost felt the release of that three pounds of pressure until some officer says you didn't see the shot he took at you and yells at you not to shoot and you hesitate to obey but he yells louder and maybe even grabs your shoulder but you don't remember because you were focused on the man in your sights' head and leading him just right so that he walks into your bullet and the slow steady squeeze waiting for the surprise bang when the rifle goes off because it should surprise you and that's how you know it's a good shot.

2. The first time you shit in a cat hole is days after you get into country because you just can't bring yourself to dig a hole like an animal and squat over it to shit in front of everybody in the middle of the desert but you have to so you do and the first thing you see is your best friend Turbo shitting in a hole a few yards from you and he waves and jokes and you wave and joke and the embed reporter drops her MOPP suit trousers and moans and shouts and her big white ass is all you can see and she mumbles about dignity and humanity and then you learn that if you knock the top and bottom out of a wooden ammo crate and put some of the foam from your ISO mat around the edge you sit on you have quite the comfy shitter.

3. When Gunny Dill who you used to call Gunnery Sergeant Dill until he made fun of you for being so formal so you shortened it to Gunny Dill or Gunny because there was no way in hell you could call him Dave like the other Sappers do loses a leg and Ray who is a Staff Sergeant and also senior to you but calls you Mikie and tells you to call him Ray loses an eye and it's the end of the deployment and they could have gone home whole but some officer told them to go clear a minefield or mark a minefield the details are a little fuzzy at night which was against Division orders but the officer said do it anyway because what about some poor Iraqi kid getting his leg blown off so Gunny Dill and Ray and Randy whose wife told him to never volunteer for anything get in a Humvee and convoy to this minefield and his first step out of the truck Gunny steps on a toe popper and sure as shit his toe pops off along with his heel and calf and Gunny gets blown clear over the Humvee deeper into the minefield and Ray takes a piece of frag in the eye and will later wear an eye patch and sometimes take out his glass eye to show kids but stayed in the Marines as long as he could and deployed as often as he could until he got medboarded out and Randy whose wife told him never to volunteer but volunteered anyway and said not to tell his wife that he

volunteered because she would kill him if she found out had a ton of frag and debris in his face and made his not-so-great skin look worse and he was wearing contacts that night and you aren't supposed to wear contacts in a war zone because the nerve gas or sarin gas or VX gas that supposedly never existed but other Marines found aimed at us but what does it matter all these years later anyhow would burn the contacts to your eyes and you would go blind which was why you wore glasses and as Randy laid on his back on an operating table after the medevac he gets cussed out by the doc pulling the frag and rocks out of his face says what the fuck and holds up a shredded contact lens and lectures Randy about wearing contacts in combat then says but it saved your eyes and next day even though we were all pretty much awake Timmy Ash in his Pacific Northwest kind of maybe a stoner before the Marine Corps voice says I wish it was me and not Gunny I mean I wish it had been me that got blown up not him isn't that fucked up RP and you say nothing because what can you say except no that isn't fucked up it makes perfect sense and it does because you feel the same way and as you make your rounds your Marines trust you to have the word and not bum scoop about Gunny and Jimmy Wining who we call Dick Fingers because well figure it out looks up with almost tears in his eyes asking if Gunny will be ok because Gunny had been his MEU platoon sergeant on deployment before the Iraq deployment and he doesn't say it but you know he would change places with Gunny if he could but he can't so he sits there on his pack cleaning his rifle with those eyes and you say Gunny is fine because he is minus the leg and he was making jokes about still being able to fuck his wife so that's a plus and then when everyone gets back to garrison and you hear Gunny Dill yelling at Gunny Toves and then Gunny Toves laughs and runs down the hall and a boot attached to a prosthetic leg has been hurled at him and it hits the wall with a thud and Gunny Dill hobbles into the hall and says what the fuck are you looking at RP and you say nothing Gunny and turn around like this is the most normal thing in the world because it is.

4. When Gunny Menusa from Bravo company is killed you were talking to the embed reporter whose ass you saw about the real price

of war is the killing and being killed and how some of the guys think it's funny but they're young and she thinks you are being profound and you aren't but she writes it all down and then you find out that Gunny took an AK round through his face and he was a lay leader and the last thing you remember of him was his face as he worshipped Jesus during a service and his son is the same age as your son and the chaplain coughs then cries and then rocks himself and you don't because he needs you right now and then when Sergeant Rios from Bravo company got killed by a sniper round through his neck and you tell Gunny Rod who used to lead him when Gunny Rod and Rios were in Charlie company and Gunny Rod cries and you put your hand on his back as you leave to give him a minute and you remember Sergeant Rios in garrison marching his guys to medical to get them shots and checkups because real Marines only go to medical to make sure they are deployable or when they've been hit and how he smiled at you that day and it was sunny and everyone remembers that smile and you remember that was early morning when you found out about Gunny and evening nautical twilight about Sergeant Rios and you can feel the cool on your skin and the wind and the dirt and the grit and the tired but for the life of you since then you can't remember what the fuck you did yesterday or where you put those goddam keys or where you put that thing ten minutes ago.

5. How parts of numbers 1, 3, and 4 are what everyone thinks the war was like but it wasn't because war is mostly waiting and sitting around and trying to sleep wherever whenever you could like the time you slept through a gun fight even though you slept next to a machine gun because sleep is a luxury and you were mostly hungry so hungry that you ate pigeons that some dead guy was raising but you hadn't eaten in days and those pigeons looked good because you hadn't eaten in days or had mail because the POGs whose job it was to deliver chow and mail were kind of afraid to come up to where you were even though where you were wasn't so bad and that guy was dead since Marines killed him and wouldn't be needing his pigeons anymore anyway and you found a stove over there by what smelled like another dead guy but you didn't go check and a propane tank

in some dirty alcove that Doc Moose carried for you because it was really fucking heavy and your hip still kind of hurt and the Laotian doc found rice and carrots and the Flip doc killed the pigeons and so you all made a stew of pigeon and rice and water and carrots and you fed the whole company and that was the time you found a pipe that had been busted open so you were able to take your first shower in about three weeks give or take and that water was so goddam cold but one of the best showers you've ever had and the whole company got to shower but no one knows about those things because those things don't make news or movies and are a little too intimate to talk about outside of the family and you are kind of tired of talking about what everyone thinks the war was like and what it was really like but you don't have anything else to talk about or more to the point anything you are interested in talking about and now that you think about it nothing really interests you anymore and this kind of worries you a little and you think that maybe this helped erode your first marriage because you didn't want to talk about anything because in the presence of real killers and real warfighters you know that your part was small and it was just a job and your biggest enemy was boredom and sandstorms but mostly boredom and so what do you really need to talk about and also what wife wants to hear that her husband had to shit in a hole or hadn't eaten or showered or slept or could kill a man but especially a child?

6. The large bomb crater where you saw a man tossing dead bodies in so you snapped a picture to remember the sight but the camera got lost and so you don't have those pictures but you still see the arm the leg and everything else and that weird grayish color that flesh turns and the blood and the bone and the smell of a dead human and how in the future some kid from the luxury of a classroom will tell you how cliché all that stuff is and he is kind of right but you still kind of want to throat punch him because isn't something only cliché if it's common and how many people have really seen that which you're sorry isn't the same as watching it in a movie or reading it in a book or being told about it and how is the I grew up and left home and went to college and then went somewhere else any less cliché but you know that's inappropriate to say or think those things so you

nod in polite silence and in your head you hear the penguin from *Madagascar* which happens to be your and your son's favorite character except for Nemo which you took him to see when you got back from Iraq because you were in Sydney and Nemo goes to Sydney and the father and son thing anyway you hear the penguin say smile and wave boys just smile and wave and that is one of the little bits of wisdom that gets you through life and keeps you out of jail though let's face it you know you wouldn't hurt anyone even though you could and even if the people who know you now even thought you thought these things they would be terrified of you.

7. The time you roll up to a Pos near dark and you hear over the radio that all the ass and air and arty and tanks and mortars have been pulled from your area but don't worry the insurgents over in the city only outnumber you two to one and will probably hit your Pos tonight so dig in and oh by the way where you are is an abandoned munitions factory and there is unexploded ordnance everywhere so be careful where you dig your holes and the CO says ok gents dig in and you repeat him and say dig in at a UXO field in the dark and he says yeah is that a problem and you say no sir and so you tell the chaplain to stay over there where it's safe while you dig the hole and your E-tool keeps hitting things that sound like metal but you can't see so you think and hope they might be rocks and every time you hear a clink your asshole tightens up just a little more and you stop and then you don't go boom so you relax and start digging again and so this goes on for a few minutes though it seem like hours which is such a cliché but finally the hole is done so you try to get some rest before the attack that may or may not come and then the Recon guys and an LAV-25 ambush the guys coming to kill you and your guys and you don't know whether to be mad that you were used as bait or that you didn't get to kill any bad guys but you really have to piss so you get up to piss and the Corpsman chief says stop and you stop in midstep and he points to all the rocks you were throwing last night and they aren't all rocks and you almost threw the not-rocks on landmines and grenades and mortar shells and artillery shells and you almost stepped on a land mine and your asshole tightens again and you back up slowly and go piss somewhere else and your friends

laugh and you laugh because what else can you do and you guys find a bunch of weapons from France and Jordan and Egypt and Italy and China and Russia and hey aren't some of these guys our allies and then you shrug because who cares at least you didn't get blown up.

8. The man with no ears and his son about the same age as yours who tells you that Saddam's secret police came in after the first war and after he said it was okay to come home because Papa Saddam loves his people and this man with no ears believed him so it was easy for the secret police to come to his house at night and wake him up and cut off his ears and execute his wife and child and you say but you have a child right there even though he is the same age as your son and you were only fourteen in the first one so this kid in front of you couldn't be this man's or this story couldn't be real and he says no this is my second child and I have more at home with my second wife after I got out of prison and he thanks you and years later you wonder if the insurgents snuck in and finally killed him for helping us or if he got to see his kids grow up like you do even though you are divorced now and your son lives with his mom on the opposite coast but hey you get to see him at Christmas and during the summer and that is better than being dead and not seeing him at all.

9. The torture chamber but also the yellowcake that some of your guys babysat for a week or so then got told didn't exist and the paintings of the US on fire and the Twin Towers on fire all of which looked a lot older than 2001 or the files that have photos and war skills of nonmilitary personnel at a training camp but you shrug because what does it matter anyway.

10. Missing the next deployment to Iraq and feeling like you've let everyone down because you're broken even though you refused a medevac in country for your stupid hip that keeps coming out of socket because you can't leave your chaplain defenseless and you can't leave without your friends and because only weaklings go to medical so you don't go until Doc makes you go and then the Corpsmen laugh at you and call you weak until they see the needle Doc sticks directly into your hip and you don't say anything at all even

when he twists the needle inside you and can feel it scrape your bone and you and the Corpsmen can hear the scrape over the sound of war machinery and then Doc tells you to turn over for the second shot and you do and the process repeats and after the Corpsmen are quiet and apologize and you take those shots every other day for a few weeks and when one of your Marines hears what you went through he hugs you and you are confused because wouldn't everybody do that because that is what Gunny Dill and Ray and Bear said the Marine Corps was like and you can't let them down and your chaplain's wife is expecting you to bring her husband home to her and her four children so how could you be a weakling and leave early and yet a few months later there you are on limited duty and ashamed to be alive and stateside because everyone else is doing more so you should be doing more but you can't because your hip keeps you home and your wife says aren't you glad to be home safe with her and your son and you aren't, well you are, but you know and you will always know what the world really looks like and that you should be out in the real world protecting the people who don't know hate or what the real world looks like but only pretend to and how being told you are safe only makes you more ashamed and you just want to be well so you can deploy again but you can barely walk but hey you have legs so don't be a little bitch and while you are broken and can't deploy you read about Fallujah and Ramadi and you die of shame for not doing your part and when you say this to outsiders they look at you like you're crazy but you know you aren't you just feel a little like Timmy or Dick Fingers and don't want any of your friends to get hurt or die or die without you or get into trouble without you but they do and as you sit at home stateside and go to sleep in a bed every night and kiss your son before he goes to school a little of you dies and cowers in shame and you read the casualty reports and too many names you know are on it and you feel powerless and ashamed that you sit at home and take your wife to the beach because no matter what anyone says you didn't earn it or at least you don't deserve it any more than anyone else does and you remember Gunny Dill and Ray before they got blown up and Bear talking about making sacrifices for the group and taking care of each other so you lie to get off limited duty so you can go back to taking care of Marines even though not one of them would ever acknowledge that you take care of them but if you have to sit in an office or put out punch and cookies on Sundays for church people one more time.

11. For being on LIMDU and getting the CASREPS and having to tell your friends who've gotten out of the Marine Corps which of your mutual friends have been killed even though you don't want to because they should get on with their lives because they've earned it but they ask so you tell them.

12. Your idea about earning it in number 11 is a direct contradiction of 10 but fuck it.

13. That you used to cry in the shower sometimes and other times in your car when you drove to campus because you missed it so much but the it you missed isn't on this list and what you missed was seeing Dave and Ray and Bear in action talking to their Marines and leading them and knowing that you'd never measure up to the leaders they were but trying in your own way like the time you went to Oki with 2/4 who'd just a few months before lost a shit ton of guys in Ramadi thirty-seven guys a record for the Iraq War that still stands and Henry and Dan and Castillo didn't pack their ponchos at the top of their pack like Bear taught you to do so when it started monsoon raining their gear was getting pretty wet pretty fast so you had them stack their packs up so you could cover them with your poncho and yeah your gear got a little bit wet but it wasn't about you or the time you were getting promoted and you told Bear and Ray and Finan and Friszell and Ryan and they came to see you get promoted and your chaplain was impressed that your Marines cared enough to come and treated you like an equal and how only Ray and Finan came to the promotion after that one because Ryan and Bear and Friszell had gotten out and Ray and Finan talked to your new Marines about you even though you had been in two other units by now and weren't a boot and it was kind of weird because you were only following their example and a million other moments like those that you won't share with anyone else but Marine family because those moments are private.

14. Even though you know it's wrong and nonsensical you will never forgive yourself for the one time you listen to your wife about getting out because she couldn't handle the stress though to be fair she did after all watch a truck fall off a bridge only she was at a friend's house watching it on TV and the truck was in Iraq and it had her friend's husband in it and so they watched him fall off the bridge and then a few days later the CACO came to tell the friend her husband was gone only she already knew because they had seen it on TV and also because you didn't really love Jesus anymore and you didn't smile and you didn't talk and you only wanted to deploy and being with her wasn't enough so for her you asked to leave the battalion since your contract was almost up and they pulled you from your third deployment which would have been back to Iraq like you were waiting for and Duncan over in Fox company says it would be great if you stayed and came with us and your Sergeant Major gets killed on that deployment and you think that if you'd been there you could have prevented it that maybe you would have seen the suicide bomber and killed the him dressed as a her because they did that over there and no one really knows about that before he blew up Sergeant Major Ellis and it mattered that your Sergeant Major was dead because he had called you a good piece of gear and you remembered the time you went to the chow hall in flip-flops which was against regs and he didn't chew your ass and you were even more embarrassed because he was civil and you felt you let him down even though he said shit like don't call him a gentleman because he was a Sergeant Major and a gentleman is someone who can measure a woman's cunt hair and not get a hard-on and you still don't even know what that means or that time during an awards ceremony for Weapons Company two Marines from Golf were whispering loudly and he shouts fifty yards across the grinder about being quiet and respectful and despite those things and in some ways because of you always remember him getting emotional when chewing some POG boot Marine's ass for being out of regs when the Marine said he was only a Marine until 1600 because Sergeant Major Ellis lived being a Marine 24/7 and the 0700–1600 Marine was something he couldn't understand and you remember him breaking his ankle and being depressed that he couldn't lead his Marines and wasn't whole and how you were so

excited that you got promoted to the SNCO ranks that you went and told him first and he chewed your ass because you said you picked up and he said you pick up trash and earn rank and is that rank trash and you said no and then he smiled and shook your hand and then you never saw him again and when he was dying and then dead you were safe in the US and another Marine a Master Guns he had known his whole life and you had a moment on the grinder in the US and you never saw Sergeant Major Ellis again because you didn't extend to go on that deployment like lots of other guys did and you wanted to but your wife wanted you to get out before you died or worse so you did.

15. That the drawing of you your son prized most is you in cammies and Kevlar with a rifle and dead bad guys on one side of the page but you also with your mouth open and eyebrows up in an angry face and it isn't until years later after close scrutiny that you notice the angry face.

16. That sometimes you used to wish you'd just been killed in Iraq which makes no sense because it wasn't really all that bad or difficult which is funny because a few years ago your ex-wife sent you a text message saying that all your old friends from your old life before anyone called you killer and for whom you would have killed then but not really now thought you had been killed there.

SLEEP

....

ON A BLACKTOP TARMAC, waiting for war we sleep. At two in the afternoon. Sunglasses and covers. Flak jackets and Kevlar in packs. Spare cammies and skivvies, socks and pictures of home in seabags. Rounds in magazines on vests. Rifles by our side. Sprawled out in order, by squads. We sleep for minutes. Until a Sergeant Major sees us. He yells. He kicks. We wake. Marines don't need sleep, he said. We need war. We need blood. We need hate. And anger. Sergeant Major made sure we had plenty.

In our Bedouin tent in Kuwait I had a spot to sleep. A corner near the door. On the hard plywood. My seabag and pack, rifle and ISO mat. No cots because the General said so. We loved the General. We would have slept on land mines if he ordered. He never did. He only said kill when the time was right. And to sleep without cots. So we did.

How can you sleep, my chaplain asks. Artillery and air make the best masseuse, I say. Embrace my rifle. Turn over. The ground heaves. Rolls. Quaking earth under my ISO mat. The desert is cold, dark, and crisp. And quiet in between war. In my sleeping bag, warmth and my rifle. Flashes in the dark sky. Gun fire. Explosions. I sleep.

IN IRAQ IN SOME TOWN IN SOME FIELD. From loudspeakers on a mosque: *(I imagine) It is your duty to kill the American infidel. God commands it. Allahu Akbar. It is your duty to kill the American infidel. God commands it. Allahu Akbar.* Sporadic AK fire. *It is your duty to kill the American infidel. God commands it. Allahu Akbar. It is your duty to kill the American infidel. God commands it. Allahu Akbar.* We need some of your Marines for an ambush, I hear one officer say to another. *It is your duty to kill the American infidel. God commands it. Allahu Akbar. It is your duty to kill the American infidel. God commands it. Allahu Akbar.* Marines gear up. Marines rush off. *It is your duty to kill the American infidel. God commands it. Allahu Akbar. It is your duty to kill the American infidel. God commands it. Allahu Akbar.* Cobras hunt overhead. *It is your duty to kill the American infidel. God commands it. Allahu Akbar. It is your duty to kill the American infidel. God commands it. Allahu Akbar.* Explosion. Automatic weapons fire. Explosion. Silence. Darkness.

It is your duty to kill the American infidel. God commands it. Allahu Akbar. It is your duty to kill the American infidel. God commands it. Allahu Akbar. It is your duty to kill the American infidel. God commands it. Allahu Akbar. It is your duty to kill the American infidel. God commands it. Allahu Akbar. I keep my boots on. Flak too. *It is your duty to kill the American infidel. God commands it. Allahu Akbar.* Pistol under my head. Rifle at my side. Toss. Turn. Sandbags under my back. Turn. Toss. *It is your duty to kill the American infidel. God commands it. Allahu Akbar. It is your duty to kill the American infidel. God commands it. Allahu Akbar.* Turn. Toss. Toss. Turn.

A BLACKTOP PARADE DECK IN BAGHDAD. My chaplain wants to sleep here. It isn't safe, I say. He doesn't want to move. Pulls rank. We stay. Gunfire. The bullets miss me by fractions of fractions of inches. We move our gear between buildings. For safety. So we can sleep. I walk to medical. Screaming. Blood. A child. A father. Blood. Screaming. Pop. I'm hit. The back of my head. My knees sag. Is this death? No blood. Confusion. Screaming. The boy's. Not mine. Marine laughs. A battery, not a bullet. A phone call. I'm going home, my brother says. Sorry, he says. Stay safe, I say. Between buildings, I roll out my ISO mat and poncho liner. I lie down and close my eyes. What a day. Grip my rifle. Toss. Turn. Turn. Toss.

Post-Iraq, in Kuwait. After convoying eighteen hours. We sleep again in a Bedouin tent. The same as before. Only different. No room. No lights. No spot for me to rack out. But mail. From home. The mail says by red light my civilian friends have moved on, gotten promoted at work, are happy. I get a nosebleed. I need a shower and sleep. Too hot. Too dusty. No clean cammies. No room to stretch. I fall asleep on top of my pack. Embrace my rifle. Toss. Turn. Turn. Toss.

On a Kuwaiti beach, after the war, waiting to go home we sleep. At ten in the morning. On the sand. In the heat. Cleanish cammies. First shower in weeks. Sunglasses and covers. No flaks, no Kevlars. Rifles by our sides. We fall out by squads, in order. Until Master Sergeant sees us. Marines don't need sleep, he says. We need war. We need—

We don't give a fuck. We get up anyway. Crowd on to LCACs like cattle in Kuwait heat. Move from shore to ship.

SHIP'S ENGINE DRONES. Pitches and rolls. Carrying us home. A lullaby. Curtain on coffin rack closes. Shuts out light. Privacy. A bed. Sheets. Bare feet and shorts. Almost Heaven. Drift off to sleep. Interrupted. RP, Marine says. You asleep? Me neither. I see their faces, RP. The ones I shot. The ones who died. The ones I killed. Blood stinks like iron. Dead bodies when they hit the ground. I miss my Sergeant. I miss Gunny. How come I only think about this at night? Scared. Scared? That little boy. That old man. The mortars. The gunfire. The grenades. The RPGs. That AMTRAC. The blood. Flesh. Bone. Our guys. Ambush. Those Cobras. The tanks. Friendly fire. How do we—? Back home. Those things. Silence. The ship's engine drones. Pitches and rolls.

BACK HOME, IN AMERICA, I [TRY TO] SLEEP. A new house. Carpet under bare feet. Clean sheets. Clean clothes. The smell of fabric softener and my four-year-old son's hair and skin. A bed. In a room. Sleep. Heaven. RPG! someone says. I'm hit, someone else says. I reach for my rifle, jump into my boots. Run downstairs. Ready to fight. What are you doing, my first wife, Jessica, says. I have no rifle. I have no boots. The RPGs, I say. Someone was hit, I say. She stares at me. Boys playing war outside, she says.

Question 11: During the past MONTH how much have you been bothered by any of the following?

	Not bothered at all	Bothered a little	Bothered alot
o. trouble sleeping	X		

YEARS LATER, IN OKINAWA, WE ROSE BEFORE DAWN ROSE, before the rooster rose, before night knew it was time to sleep. We got our rifles, fell in by squads on the armory blacktop. And slept for minutes. Then we woke, and marched miles. A ditch. A stop. We're resting, Staff Sar'nt said. Get 'em down, he said. In the ditch. We slept. Some on this side, some on that, facing one another in the ditch. Sitting. It had rained hours earlier. The ditch was still wet. We slept. We woke. We marched again.

You take the high ground, I told the chaplain. It was raining. Had rained. Every day. For the last eighteen. The Marines dug holes that filled up with rain when they slept. Filled up with rain while they dug the holes. When they drained the holes. It rained. Only Marines go to the field during the rainy season. Because we're Marines. Because we are hard. It makes us better killers.

We are better killers. We don't need tents. I have a poncho. The chaplain has his. We tie them together. Lash them to four stakes. We sleep. The rain beats the taut ponchos. Taps. Tattoo. We sleep. I wake. To water. Not rain. Weight on my chest. Moisture. Inhale plastic. My bare feet free. Chest confined. I cannot move. I shout. I kick. The XO laughs. I am buried. Under my poncho and rainwater. My rifle is wet. My T-shirt is wet. My blouse, my trousers, my boots, and spare dry clothes, all wet. The chaplain was dry. He laughed, too.

BACK HOME IN AMERICA, I [TRY TO] SLEEP. Another new house. Carpet on bare feet. Clean sheets. Television voices and canned laughter. White noise. No rifle by my side. Quiet. Peace. Toss. Turn. Turn. Toss.

Question 11: During the past MONTH how much have you been bothered by any of the following?

	Not bothered at all	Bothered a little	Bothered alot
o. trouble sleeping	X		

ON A FIELD OP ON PENDLETON IN THE CHAPEL TENT we [try to] sleep. The [a different] chaplain and I. It is cold. My rifle by my side. Our homes minutes away. We have cots. Cold air blows underneath the cots. Seeps through the seams in the cavernous tent. Cools the tent even more. Both of us have slept in worse. The cold is unbearable. We talk. About Iraq. He wishes I had been his RP. Fallujah. Kicking in doors. Take the city. Artillery. Gunfire. Explosions. Sleep two minutes here, five there. Kicking in more doors. Take more of the city. How it is funny. Warriors spend their lives wanting to get shot at. Shoot at others. After. Realize we could have done without it. Move on. Toss. Turn. Teeth chatter. Turn. Toss. Shiver. Sleep.

AT HOME I [TRY TO] SLEEP. Carpet on bare feet. Clean sheets. No rifle by my side. Television voices and canned laughter. White noise. Quiet. Peace. Toss. Turn. Turn. Toss.

At home I [try to] sleep. Carpet on bare feet. Clean sheets. No rifle. Television voices and canned laughter. White noise. Quiet. Peace. Toss. Turn. Turn. Toss. Sergeant Major died today. Exsanguination from explosion. I wasn't there. For me: Carpet on bare feet. Clean sheets. Quiet. Peace. I wasn't there. Toss. Turn. Turn. Toss.

At home I [try to] sleep. Carpet on bare feet. Clean sheets. Television voices and canned laughter. White noise. Quiet. Peace. Where is my rifle? Toss. Turn. Turn. Toss. Gunny calls. He missed this deployment, too. Rookie is dead. I failed him, he says. He cries. I listen. I hang up. In the darkness I [try to] sleep. Gunny cried. Quiet. Peace. Toss. Turn. Turn. Toss. Where is my rifle? Gunny cried. Toss. Turn. Turn. Toss.

Question 11: During the past MONTH how much have you been
bothered by any of the following?

	Not bothered at all	Bothered a little	Bothered alot
o. trouble sleeping		X	

12. a. Over the PAST MONTH, what major life stressors have you
experienced that are a cause of significant concern or make it difficult
for you to do your work, take care of things at home, or get along with
other people (for example, serious conflicts with others, relationship
problems, or a legal, disciplinary, or financial problem)?

None or Please list and explain: I am leaving my unit. My wife and I
are divorcing.

NEW APARTMENT QUIET AT NIGHT. I [try to] sleep. Annapolis, not Camp Pendleton. No wife, no son. No rifle. No Marines to call. Just me. Alone. Make some tea. Add lots of whiskey. Fall asleep in armchair. Repeat.

No forms asking if I have trouble sleeping.

NO MORE SERVICE. I [try to] sleep. I lie down. Close my eyes. Clean sheets. Clean bed. Quiet. New wife, Lisa, not rifle by my side. Peace. Sergeant Major. Rookie. Gunny. Sergeant times 3. Corporal times 4. Lance Corporal times I can't remember. Doc. Twenty-two vets a day. Toss. Turn. Turn. Toss. Sergeant Major. Rookie. Gunny. Sergeant times 3. Corporal times 4. Lance Corporal times I can't remember. Doc. Twenty-two vets a day. Toss. Turn. Turn. Toss.

New wife [tries to] sleep[s] next to me. She lies down. Closes her eyes. Clean sheets. Clean bed. New husband not rifle by her side. Ramadi, Iraq. Rockets. Explosions. Shrapnel hits wall. Rocket destroys can. Sergeant Major saves from RPG. Bomb kills friend. I hear her whimper, run for cover. I feel her: Toss. Turn. Turn. Toss.

AGOGE

January 2014. Victorville, California.

Taps. A moment of silence for the men and women who have sacrificed themselves for their country. I stand. I am the only one standing. The high school auditorium filled with parents of graduating Young Marines remains quiet, as Taps calls to us from PA speakers, but no one stands. They don't know any better. No one teaches them.

My son. Fourteen years old, in woodland-patterned cammies. Black leather boots and eight-point cover. He stands, marches front and center. Reading of a meritorious promotion warrant. Handshake. Left face. March two paces. Right face. Handshake. Private First Class chevron placed on the right collar, then the left. Handshake. Hand salute. Left face. Forward march.

I want to enlist in the Marine Corps for real, he says. I want to be a grunt, he says. Even after everything, I say. Yes, he says.

Marines in formation. No one has died in battle in a long time.

Me. Twenty-six years old and wearing woodland rip-stop cammies. Black leather boots and eight-point cover. Forward march. I march front and center. Hand salute. Reading of a meritorious promotion warrant. Handshake. My son. Three years old in his mother's arms. Company Commander helps the toddler place a chevron on my right collar. Handshake. Hand salute. Left face. Forward march.

After the ceremony, when the officers have left and my son and wife walked out of the room, my friends close the door to my office and lock it, remove the brass backs of my chevron. Sharp metal prongs separated from skin by fabric. Welcome to the Marine Corps, Greensider, they say. Their fists drive the points of my chevrons into my chest. I bleed. They knee me in the thigh. We smile.

Proud father. Proud son. He looks like me. He is taller than me. New cammies. Black leather boots. I tell him to take his cover off indoors. We don't do that, I say. He removes his cover without question.

Be nice, my mom says. He's just a kid, my sisters say. The agoge, I say.

In Sparta, boys were taken from their mothers between ages six and eight and placed in military training. Beatings. Fights. Marching. Beatings. Fights. Weapons. Tactics. Marching. Men teaching boys to take their place in the line.

He's six years behind, I say.

These are our customs, my son says. My mom and sisters stare at us.

Give me a quarter, I say. No one questions. My mother gives me one. I take the quarter, place it on my son's collar. Use the quarter to place your chevrons, I say. I learned this from my seniors. Now I've taught you. Understood? Yes dad, he says.

I pretend to remove the backs of his chevrons. He smiles. Shiny prongs of metal separated from skin by fabric, he thinks. I make two fists and hammer strike his chevrons. No blood. I smile. So does he. We hug.

Me. Thirty years old. Digital-pattern cammies. Tan suede boots and eight-point cover. White walls with unit crests of each regiment in the division. Forward march. I march front and center. Hand salute. Reading of a promotion warrant. Handshake. My son. Seven years old, wearing khakis and a white polo shirt, marches front and center. He stands at the position of attention next to the Battalion Commander. BC hands my son my new chevron. I take a knee as he places it on my collar as best he can. My son makes a fist, raises it, strikes my chevron with all his might, trying to draw blood. Formation of Marines, his surrogate fathers and older brothers laughs. BC speechless. Handshake. Hand salute. Left face. Forward march. I want to smile but can't.

Me. Thirty-seven years old. In my mother's living room. My mother and father and sisters watching me and my son.

Lay the trousers flat on their side, I tell him, fold them so a natural crease forms. Fold the top leg back, press the bottom leg. Lots of steam, lots of pressure make a sharp crease. Repeat for the other leg. Do this until the crease is ironed in. The crease is important.

Here is your cammie blouse, I say. Iron the pockets flat, press the sleeves. I take his hand and put it under mine. Guide his hand over his uniform. This is your uniform. A link in the chain of our history. Wear it with pride and make sure it looks sharp. Don't fail the men who've worn this before you. Understood? Yes dad, he says.

Hang your cammies up, I say, careful not to disturb the creases. Take your fingernail clippers and a lighter. Trim or burn all the IPs. No stray threads. This is how we take care of our uniforms. Understood? Yes dad, he says.

Give me a credit card, I say. My sisters sacrifice two of theirs. Cut it like so, I say, and place one in the front of the cover, the other in the back. See how it gives the cover shape? Yes, dad.

He won't learn if you help him, my dad says. It's our way, I say, someone has to teach him.

Me. Twenty-six years old wearing desert boots and desert cammies. A crowded, yellow-plastic-walled Bedouin tent that reeks of dirty feet and body odor and cardboard mustiness of MRE and water boxes and the choking dryness of Kuwaiti desert sand.

Mail call. A letter. From my father. I stare at it a moment. Wonder why my father has sent me a letter. We never spoke at home. The envelope is wrinkled and desiccated from the desert sandy dust.

I admire you son, and I'm proud of you, my father's letter says. Your grandpa landed at Anzio, your uncle Bobby was in the Navy, my cousin was in the Marines during Vietnam, and I didn't have the balls to enlist. I didn't have to go, but I could have. I should have, but I didn't. You and your brother did, and I don't know where you are or if you two have seen each other. I wanted to let you know I am proud of you and that you are a better man than I am.

I fold the letter back up and put it in my cargo pocket. I walk over to my rack and look at the picture of my son, a toddler, in the webbing of my helmet.

I never want to tell my son I was a coward.

I look around the tent, I hear the machinery of war, I don't want this for my son.

My son and I sit cross-legged on my mother's living room floor. A pair of black leather jungle boots on a towel in front of us. Brush your boots first, I say. Take a corner of the T-shirt, rub it in the polish. Take the polish and rub gently, in small circles, into the leather. Small circles, slow at first, I repeat. I demonstrate. The motion creates friction, opens up the leather's pores. Allows the polish to seep in, builds a good foundation. Now you try.

He takes a boot. Applies the polish in large circles. Quick. Sloppy. Wrong.

No, I say. Look. I repeat my demonstration. It must be done this way. I take his hand in mine and show him the way. Pressure, I say. Small circles, I say. Start at the tip of the boot, work in a pattern. Take your time. Get it right. How can you lead, be an example, if you can't get the basics. You have rank. Others will look to you.

Can't he take a break, my mom says. He just graduated, my sisters say, a kid. Let him have some fun. My father says nothing. The women of Sparta used to tell their men, while handing them their shields as the men got ready to march for battle, Either with this or on this. Come back victorious or come back dead. Sometimes I wish we were Sparta. I wouldn't have to explain anything.

No, I say. I don't have enough time. Who else will show him?

Me. Twenty-eight years old. My living room. A Sunday afternoon.

Want to polish boots with me? My four-year-old son says yes. He watches for five seconds, runs around the house. He wants to play. So do I, but I have responsibilities.

I sit on the living room floor, cross-legged, my black leather jungle boots on a towel in front of me. I dip a T-shirt in black polish, apply it in small circles starting at the tip of the boot. First one boot, then the other. Ninety minutes pass. Perfection. I place the spit-polished boots on the towel; both boots like mirrors.

My son stands in front of my boots with his shoes on. He smiles. Picks up his toddler foot and slams his shoe onto the toe of my freshly polished boot, laughs, and runs away.

My son and I stand in my mother's entryway. He is in uniform. I am in civilian clothes. Ah-ten-hut, I say. He comes to the position of attention. Feet at forty-five-degree angles, body straight, hands at side, curled into fists, thumbs along the seams of his trousers. Head and eyes front. The basic position. The starting position. No, I say. I correct his hand and thumb placement. I kick my foot between his two, to demonstrate the proper angle. Back straight, I say, chest out. My mother, my father, my two sisters watch us.

You're okay with him doing this, my sister says. With enlisting? Even after everything you and Nick have been through. She starts to cry. So does my mom. Yes, I say. My son is still at attention.

Forty inches front to back, I say. Left. Face. The distance your brother should be in front of and behind you. Forty inches at all times. I take my place in line, in front of him. Take your cover off; hold it, arm outstretched. I back step until the cover touches my shirt. See the distance? Yes, dad. Remember it, I say. Forty inches, he says. Front to back.

How, my sister says. Why. Because, I say. This is what men do. I am a warrior. It is right for him to be, too. And it's his decision, I say. He has heard the stories. Seen the after. It won't be easy. But his mind is made up.

Right. Face, I say. We move in unison to the right. I am beside him. Right face. In unison we pivot to the right. I am behind him. Shoulders back. Head straight. Stare into nothing. Yes, dad.

Marching, I say. Close order drill. This is vital. We have marched since ancient times. Thousands of years. The warrior who can march with his brothers wins battles. The warriors who cannot march lose battles. Understood? Yes, dad, my son says. We will practice.

Together. Remember to step off with the left foot, I tell him. Always the left foot. Yes, dad. Forward. March. I fall in line behind him. I call the cadence. Your left. Right. Left. Right. Left. We turn around. He is behind me. We march together, take turns leading and following until he can do it without me.

PART TWO

RED SHOES

In the Archers' '48 film *The Red Shoes*, Vicky Page wants to be a dancer. Dancing consumes her. The red shoes consume her. In the end she dies and asks Julian Craster to take the red shoes off. But before all that dancing, Julian the aspiring musician tells Boris Lermontov the opera impresario that his professor stole the music for Boris's opera. Boris offers Julian a job and tells Julian this: It is worth remembering that it is much more disheartening to have to steal than to be stolen from, hmmm?

I remember that movie, that scene, when I see the man in Marine cammies on a Sunday coming out of the buffet in my town. I see that man wearing a uniform he probably didn't earn because if he had earned it, he wouldn't be wearing it because Marines don't wear cammies in public, and then I think, I think of the poser I met on a walk, then see in line for a free Veterans Day meal, and then I think about every other poser I have seen.

Sometimes I am Boris. I feel bad that someone needs to wear a fake uniform and tell fake stories for people to like him. Go ahead. Wear the uniform, make up stories, get free stuff. That's all we are. A uniform with cool stories that gets discounts and freebies. I mean, that's why we all joined, right?

Sometimes I am Boris because I know that they know they're thieves and cowards. Weak and pathetic. Too afraid to volunteer during the Long War but happy to get handouts and cheap hero worship.

Other times I am Julian. I am angry and I want justice.

I am angry and want justice because they couldn't even do a Google search on uniform regs. At least try to look the part. Do you have any idea how big a pain in the ass it is to make sure everything is squared away, how hard shaving every day is on the skin, how expensive haircuts and medals and ribbons are? And because they don't just hand out uniforms and ribbons and medals like candy. We had to earn that shit. And sometimes the earning wasn't worth the cost.

Other times I am Julian because fuck you.

Fuck you that we're just a uniform with cool stories and a free meal or appetizer on Veterans Day.

Fuck you because you don't know that when I see you parading around in a uniform you didn't earn I see every man I ever knew who did earn it and paid for it in blood and you're pissing on them. And fuck you because you don't know we hate being called hero. That being thanked is awkward and strange because we were just doing our job and we didn't die when others did. And fuck you when you talk about Americana and freedom because the truth is we didn't do it for them or you but for the man on our left and the man on our right and what are people thanking us for anyway? Do they even know?

And fuck you because you don't know those cool stories and uniforms come with waking dreams and sometimes therapy and sometimes VA candy or sometimes nothing at all but confidence and quiet and—

You know what? Never mind.

But then I am Boris again and I wonder if maybe those are the only clothes that man has, because why else would anyone wear cammies after they got out? I realize that maybe I am an asshole, that maybe it isn't that serious.

But when I see someone in uniform or telling fake stories it enrages me, like the rage of Achilles, the rage memorialized for millennia, the rage that *killed* him, which makes me think that maybe I am not Boris, I am not even Julian. I am Vicky.

I am Vicky and all I can see are the red shoes. All I want is to dance, or remember the dance. Which is why I rewatch YouTube videos from the old days when I am having a bad day—that video, the Seether one—just to hear the sound of belt feds and ass and the pop pop pop of a rifle, the movement to contact, Marines exploding into a room, to get the blood moving, to feel anything besides the lethargy of this new civilian existence, to recapture even for a moment the exhilaration of being alive, the grief of surviving, the beauty of a cigarette after someone fails to kill you.

I am Vicky, and maybe that's why my old cammies and combat boots are in a footlocker and I can't get rid of them. Those combat boots were all I ever wanted, all that ever mattered, and after a divorce and therapy, and waking dreams and nightmares and homesickness, I still have them. Rationalize wearing them after a hurricane or to do work around the house. Remember feeling like my identity had been stolen when I had to take off the cammies and boots and put on the air conditioner repairman suit, then a dress uniform, then civvies.

And maybe we are all Vicky and that's part of the reason so many of us kill ourselves. That we are all of us consumed by the dance and we don't know how to take the shoes off to save our lives, or maybe we don't want to take the shoes off. The fear of the unknown is too great, life without the dance, and the music too boring, and so we dance, and keep the shoes on.

But what if we take them off? What if I take them off before I end up like Vicky? What happens then?

HEARSAY

(Note: When you see _____ insert the name of a vet you know or at least someone you care about)

Only the dead have seen the end of war, Plato says. At least we think so. Because like so many things about war, we only heard about it. We heard it from a guy who knew a guy, who knew the guy whose friend knew the guy that knew the guy who heard it first.

Like when we heard about _____ who killed himself. We weren't there, but we found out from a Marine who heard it from another Marine who saw it on the news. So we're left to wonder. Had he had enough? Did he want to see the end of war? Or was he just tired?

Because they always call you in the middle of the night when you're sleeping after telling you to go back to your barracks room or your wife and child. Take a few days to relax before this pump, they always say. Our window isn't for a few days, they say, but you've deployed before and you know the game, but you go home anyway because what the hell else are you gonna do? So you go home and look at the seabag in the corner, take your wife out to dinner, and neither of you speak and neither of you taste anything and then maybe you fight because it's easier to say good-bye that way and then at night the phone rings and get up, they say, we're leaving, be on the grinder at zero dark thirty.

You can never really sleep after a phone call like that. So you show up with your gear and put your green seabag in a row and put your pack in a row and then get in formation and march to the armory to stand in line and laugh and joke and curse because you are there fifteen minutes prior to fifteen minutes prior to fifteen fucking minutes prior and the armory isn't even open yet, and your flak is heavy and the strap to your Kevlar is twisted on your plate carrier and your gear gets heavier and you're standing in line and then you have your weapon and your pointy green-tipped bullets and you march back to the grinder and your toddler son tries to grab your Ka-Bar bayonet and he thinks it's cool that you have a bayonet and rifle and pistol and you hope he never has to do this but in the future he will tell you he wants to enlist like you did but before all that you get on the busses that sit for an hour as your family looks at you at the edge of the grinder and you kind of wish they would just leave so you could just leave and then you go and wait some more and then you go and come back.

And you can never really fall asleep after a deployment like that so maybe _____was just tired and that's why he killed himself. But before he kills himself he gets out and says I'm going to go to school on the Post-9/11 GI Bill and make a life for myself because haven't I earned it?

Only no one at TAPS told him how hard it would be. Sure, they thanked him for his service and taught him how to dress for a job interview and told him to say please and thank you and quit saying fuck so much, but they didn't tell him how much America had changed, why would they tell an American that America was different, didn't he live here? They didn't tell him how much he had changed, they only told him to take off his uniform and forget about the past, who he was, and try to get some rest, transition, they say, only he can't forget his past and he isn't even sure he wants to and he can't get some rest but he goes to bed and wakes and goes to class. And he gets more and more tired.

But he isn't ever really thinking about killing himself, just how tired he is. Tired of transition, tired of school, tired of being unemployed, tired of not having any money because Congress changed the terms of the Post-9/11 GI Bill and so he only has eight dollars left in his checking account since he is unemployed and when he called the prior service recruiter so he could go home and get some rest they said thanks but no thanks, you're old and broken and we don't want tattooed combat vets we want young fresh recruits, and he isn't sure how to feed his wife and kids or pay his bills, all of which means he is failing as a man and failure isn't good because failure in his world means death. But we don't fail, we adapt, we improvise, we overcome. But you aren't transitioning and they keep saying transition but you can't, so it's you not them and you know that failing means death, but you don't want to die, you just want some rest, but you can never really rest after that time you almost got shot in the face or that time you thought you'd gotten shot in the head but it was just a Comm battery knocking you unconscious, but you can't think like that because that's how you try to kill yourself.

So instead of killing himself he gets counseling at the VA and they ask him why he's there and they want to talk about stuff he'd rather not talk about it which is dumb that they ask because everyone is always telling him to move forward—but they always want to bring up all that old shit—and he's trying to move forward but it's just not working, and school is going well but he and his wife just aren't. And the VA doc asks him if he is feeling guilt and shame for what he has done for his country and he says don't be stupid he didn't do it for his country he did it for the guy on his left and right and he's a warrior why would he feel shame, but this isn't the first time he's heard that so maybe yeah it is a little bit of shame and guilt, it had just never occurred to him, and he leaves and gets lots of VA drugs in the mail, enough to drug a whole city, and he's forgotten who he is, that he is a warrior, because he only was a warrior because everyone told him was not is and now he's ashamed because the civilians he knows would feel shame and so now he's no longer a warrior just an ashamed has-been with eight dollars in his bank account and a plummeting credit score and so maybe that's why finally he rented car or posted a good-bye on Facebook or didn't say anything, and

then you hear from a Marine who heard it from a Marine that _____
is dead because he killed himself.

And you wonder how it happened and you wonder if he just wanted
to go home and you wonder if he finally got some sleep. And you
wonder if he finally knows the end of war.

And you wonder before he pulled the trigger if he took the barrel
of his pistol out of his mouth like you did because he didn't like the
taste of CLP either.

ONTARIO AIRPORT, TERMINAL FOUR

....

Ontario Airport, Terminal Four, is where I left from to go to Field Med School after I came home on boot leave. I didn't have much leave and it was over and I had a school to get to. Orders. My son was two. He was buckled into his car seat when my wife and her mother dropped me off. My son had never been to the airport before. As I got out of the vehicle to go to my flight my son reached for me and cried. He knew I was leaving. When I say cried, I mean screamed. And he reached for me and said Daddy.

But I had to go. And it was hard. He was my little football. When I was a civilian, I worked graveyard at a grocery store, and when I came home around five or so I would go to his crib first thing and wake him up if he wasn't already awake. I would play with him or change him or pick him up and carry him tucked into my right fore-arm like a football. He was small enough for that then. Before I left for boot camp, I made him a video so he could hear my voice and watch it whenever he missed me. My wife said he played the video over and over again and that it calmed him down.

And then I came back and now I was leaving him at the airport to get trained for my job protecting chaplains with Marine infan-try. I hugged him to quiet him and then I said I had to go. I held back my tears, grabbed my seabag, and went to my flight. That was 2002.

Ontario Airport, Terminal Four, is where he would fly from to come see me. I divorced his mom in 2008 and had orders to the Naval Academy. After a trip to Iraq and a long time with Marines she said I wasn't the boy she married and I wasn't so we split up.

The day I told my son, he and I went to the San Diego Zoo together. It was overcast and cold, which was odd for September in SoCal. We got hot chocolate by the reptile house, and he was wearing a brown Vans T-shirt and tan cargo shorts.

He was excited to be spending time with me, he was excited to be at the zoo, and he was excited that we had orders, and then over hot chocolate I told him that his mom and I were getting a divorce. Oh, he said. Well, he said, I can still come visit Mom when we leave, right? No, I said. You will be staying with Mom for now. A little boy needs his mom, I said. I said this because I couldn't say that his mom refused to get a divorce unless I left my son with her even though she said I wasn't the person she married anymore. But when you are thirteen, I said, come live with me, and until then I'll fly you out every chance I get, and we will go on trips and do all the things we like and find new things to like.

He took a sip of hot chocolate and his eyes got teary and then he said, well lots of my friends from school's parents are divorced. I can just pretend like you are on deployment again, he said. I told him I was sorry. I told him it wasn't his fault and that his mom and I love him very much. I asked if he was okay. He told me he would be and that he loved me and then we went and saw the reptiles and the elephants and wolves and tigers and rode the sky buckets and the tram and saw the rest of the animals at the zoo. So does this mean I get two birthdays and two Christmases, he said.

Ontario Airport, Terminal Four, is where I flew into for my brother's wedding in 2011. My mom and my sisters told me that they'd pick me and my fiancée up from the airport, but I guess they forgot because when I called to tell them we'd arrived and asked where they were, they told me they were bowling. I got angry and rented a car and booked a hotel room and then left my fiancée in it while I went and picked up my son from his mother. But before that, when I walked off the plane into the terminal, I remembered my first time at Ontario Airport and how my son cried and I told my fiancée about it.

Ontario Airport, Terminal Four, is where I flew into to watch my son's Young Marines graduation in 2014. The summer before he told me wanted to join the real Marines. Ever since he was a kid, he said. He grew up on Camp Pendleton, knew all my friends, heard all our stories, and we taught him how to clear houses and rush a target and how to dig a fighting hole because he loved to play war like we did only we weren't playing. Go to college first, I said. Then join, even if you don't want a commission, I said. He laughed and said no. I hate school, he said. Besides, he said. We don't have money for me to go to college and since I don't want to go anyway what's the point of going into debt. After I enlist, I will have earned my own college money and I can go to college after I am out if I want, he said. Going to college after the military is hard, I said. You went to college after the military, he said. I know and it was hard going back and dealing with kids you have nothing in common with and I am telling you it's easier to go to college first, I said. But you did it and now you almost have a Master's degree. If you can do it, then I can do it, too.

I was surprised when his mom texted and told me she put him in Young Marines because she was against him joining. She was in fact antimilitary after our divorce and then she said she put him in Young Marines and I figured it was to keep him out there with her since we wanted him to come live with us and he told her he wanted to come live with us and then after joining Young Marines he said he would stay in California.

So I flew to his graduation where his Gunny told me how well he did and after meeting me and shaking my hand told me that now my son being good at PT and military bearing and the intangible values made sense since well, you know his mother and it didn't come from her. And I was proud of my son and he got meritoriously promoted and then I helped him learn drill and take care of his uniform and then I flew back to North Carolina from Ontario Airport, Terminal Four.

Ontario Airport, Terminal Four, is where I flew into to attend his high school graduation in 2017. His graduation was on the Wednesday before Memorial Day weekend. He enlisted in the Marine Corps on his seventeenth birthday as an 03xx. An infantryman. A grunt. A killer. I am proud of him. More proud of him for enlisting than graduating high school because I think, as he does, that it isn't anything more than the bare requirement to be an adult. He leaves for boot camp in San Diego at the end of this August. Our plan is for he and I to fly home and then return in July for my sister's wedding, then he will stay in California and ship to boot camp at the end of August.

Everyone—my mom, dad, sisters (but not my Iraq vet brother), civilian friends (outsiders)—keeps asking me how I feel about it, him enlisting, they mean. After everything am I okay with him enlisting, they ask. Am I scared is what they mean. They ask in code so they don't have to admit their own fear. I see a lot of that type of projection, but that's another discussion for another time. All the questions remind me of when I enlisted and everyone asked if I was sure and then after 9/11 how everyone kept asking if I was sure about enlisting and hinting that maybe I should try to get out of my contract. I remember one time a man I knew, a coworker, told me I should join the Reserves so I wouldn't be near any danger or fighting. That in the Reserves it was easy. All I would have to do is a BS duty on the weekend once a month and two weeks once a year and I'd get paid and get some bennies. But I wanted to fight so I thought he was a coward and I told him so. Guys don't like being called cowards when they are. Weird. So no, I am not afraid. For me or my son.

Before we fly home I arrange to meet Ray, a brother from 1st CEB for a (pre-) Memorial Day hike up First Sergeant Hill. I invite Paschall, a brother from 2/4, and I am excited because I haven't been home to Pendleton or seen them in nine years. My son is excited because he hasn't been home since then either. We get in my soon-to-be-brother-in-law's car and drive the 15 South to Mission Road and we recognize all the landmarks that we used to pass on our way home. There are new buildings but enough old ones that I feel the old feelings. We stop at the McDonald's outside the gate where we used to stop nine years ago, the one inside the gas station in the Ralph's shopping center. It smells the same and feels the same, I say about the Pendleton air. Yeah, he says. Weird that we remember. Just like old times.

But it isn't old times. My son is seventeen and I am forty-one. And First Sergeant Hill doesn't have any ropes anymore. And there isn't anyone telling us to get up the mountain, so Ray and Goat and Joe and David and Mueller and I struggle up that damn mountain. I think Goat pukes once. The beer didn't help. Paschall is still Active so it isn't as difficult for him. My son runs up the mountain. Twice. At a plateau on the mountain, I check my phone and see that my son texted me asking what he should do. I said wait for us. But he had already made it to the top so he ran back down. And waited. He ran back up to the top where the memorials are because he got tired of waiting for us. We all had a beer. And then we left. And then for the first time, my son and I fly home together out of Ontario Airport, Terminal Four, the next day.

Ontario Airport, Terminal Four is where I fly out of, alone, the morning after my sister's wedding and my son stays behind to go to boot camp. When I wake up I realize that this is it. I've watched it happen all summer long. Time slipping away. Him slipping away, leaving.

I've watched all summer Marines I know, Marines I've just met, welcome him to the family with a raised glass or bottle and a hug or a handshake. The Marines swap sea stories and include him and give him advice on boot camp, the Fleet. They ask if he can have a drink with us, and I allow, and they treat him like one of their own. Like they treat me. And the Marines don't ask if I'm scared or worried like civilians do. They hug me and smile and talk about how proud I must feel and they share my pride. Even when the stories turn grave and the talk turns serious, we are proud uncles and a father.

And I have watched, all summer, outsiders dispense their boot camp wisdom and pointers even though they've never been. I watch these outsiders try to be profound and connect with my son, and I watch him politely not roll his eyes but catch mine as if it to say is this what it's like for you and what it will be like for me. I look him in the eyes back. Yes it is and will be.

I think, in that moment between wakefulness and movement, about all these things: the separations, the pride, the outsiders who know without ever experiencing, and I think about my son at seventeen. I think about all these things and my flight ahead in the shower alone, getting dressed, and as he and I stand in front of the hotel bathroom mirror brushing our teeth.

We rinse and then we are silent. This is it, I say. The next time I see you, you'll be a Marine. Yes, he says. Another moment of silence. We walk into the living area in front of the mirror. You know, I say, at times like this people think you have to say some parting words of wisdom or maybe a fatherly blessing or something like that. But one of the many things the Marine Corps has taught me and will teach you is that that's a lie, I say. Those moments aren't real. And often those words aren't either, I say. I have no final words, I say. All I can say is that I love you, that I am proud of you and the man you are becoming. He is silent while I say these things until he says, I love you too, Dad. And then I hug him there in front of the mirror in that hotel room. We must have looked funny because he is nearly three inches taller than me, maybe more, and as I hugged him tight, it's the first time I notice how much taller than me he is.

After we let go of our hug we grab our gear and walk in silence to the elevator and down to the lobby and out to the street where my sister the maid of honor, not my sister the bride, waits for us. We load our gear in her small car and she drives us to the airport. Ontario Airport. Terminal Four. The place where I left him and he cried for me not to leave. Only now when I get out of the car, he gets out, too, and helps me with my bags and gives me a final hug before I turn and walk into that same terminal and up those same stairs away from him like I did so many years ago.

SITTING

It's going to be weird to be sitting today, I say to Lisa. We should be standing, in formation, where they will be, I say.

That time has passed.

They are all so young, she says. I say the same thing: they are all so young. That officer, did his mom give him a note to be here, we say. We are so old, I say. The ceremony will begin shortly, please take your seats, HM1 says. We, the old and grizzled and maybe even fat guests, look at each other. We long to move into formation with the Corpsmen. But we haven't any uniforms, and we have face hair, except my wife, who, of course, shouldn't, and we have some extra pounds and the HM1 again asks us to sit. We all of us out-of-uniform old-timers—old-timers! at forty-one or thereabouts—snicker as the HM1 waits for us to sit. I have never sat at one of these things before, some old SMAJ—I'm guessing—says loud enough for all of us to hear or perhaps not but a once SMAJ or whatever isn't used to speaking soft.

How did we get here, I wonder. Under the sun, so many years removed from Iraq or Afghanistan. The sun. It is bright and warm and it passes through the trees and illuminates the marble memorial for all of Wolfpack's—2nd LAR's—KIA. Beatific. Illuminated.

Warming the cold stone. There are many names on that stone. There are many names on stones just like it across the Corps and Greenside Navy, those names foreign to me, are the same names as those I know, that everybody like us knows. We are here for one name today, for HM3 Benjamin P. Castiglione. For Ben. For Stiggy. For Doc.

But how did we get here? We drove.

Tommy, who died the same day Stiggy did, from what I was told, but came back and didn't die or maybe just nearly died, invited us to the BAS dedication. One of Lisa's squidlets was married to Tommy then when he got hit, and Lisa and Tommy had worked together and she felt it was her place to come. It is. And it is mine as her husband and a friend and brother of Tommy's.

Come pick up your base pass from the house, he said in a Facebook message. Here's the address. Rah, I said. I expected it to be his house or a friend's house or some other house, but the house where Doc's family was staying for the weekend? The house where Doc's family came from Michigan to Atlanta to here or just Michigan to here or Arizona to here and stayed? I didn't expect that. I wasn't prepared. I never am. Prepared to meet the family, that is. No one ever is, I think. Until you meet, and then they accept you a proxy son or daughter. Not to replace but to augment, to keep immortal, their child.

Doc died on September 3, 2009, in Afghanistan. Today is November 3, 2017. Today, the men hug each other. Make jokes about weight. Catch up on the last few years. Look at the memorial. My office is now the bathroom, one Doc said. Figures, he said. I swear that MO is barely twenty-one, a retired Senior Chief says. And the men. They cluster. They hug more. They laugh. They fall silent. And then we sit. And then the ceremony starts.

The chaplain prays. A chaplain always prays, and the Muslims, Jews, Christians, Hindus, Buddhists, Atheists, whatever religion in uniform bow their head not because religion is king or they were forced to or any civilian myth bullshit like that but because it's respect, reverence. For each other, for the dead. For the holy wonder of life and death. Amen, the chaplain says, and we sitting say amen or we say nothing and the men in uniform in unison raise their heads.

Doc Camacho and Tommy, HMCS Peterson as it were, speak. They speak about Doc, about Ben. They choke up, maybe more than they speak, and no one judges. These are our moments. Private. Sacred. These moments are never easy no matter the number of years gone by.

Tommy looks at we who are sitting, thanks Doc's mom and Stiggy for looking out for him, then he says something not surprising. When he left the Wolfpack, when he left home, the demons came, he said. It's unsurprising because I have long suspected it's the leaving that hurts the most, makes the moving forward the hardest for warfighters. Because the guy you looked to for a smartass reality check isn't within arm's reach or a shout. Because the guy who loves you and you love isn't there and neither are the ones who remember. The strength of the pack is the wolf and the strength of the wolf is the pack, they say at Wolfpack. It's true everywhere. Tommy charges the Corpsmen in the formation to model Stiggy's example. Teach your Marines how to save lives, learn how to take lives, and love one another.

The sun is still warm and the crowd is still silent and still we wonder how did we get here? How was it not us but him? Or them? How? How? How? There isn't an answer. There is only action. I am here. We are here. We had better be here. Be present in the moment and breathe deep and soak up the warm sun and love as fierce as we fought.

A Doc brings the shadow box forward. Another Doc brings Stiggy's mother flowers. And just like that the BAS is dedicated in honor of Doc HM3 Ben Stiggy Castiglione.

We rise, those of us sitting who once used to be standing. We rise in silence. And the silence is loud as the sun is warm, if even for a moment. The boot Docs stay in formation a few seconds before they leave, some thinking about what Tommy said, the responsibility they bear. And we who used to stand but now sit do what people like us do, have always done. Catch up. Laugh. Hug. Talk shit. And gather our things and walk in the warm sun.

41: A MEDITATION

40 + 1. 4 × 10 + 1. A number, the number.

The number of years between 1966 and 2007.

The number of years between 1976 and 2017.

The number of years when time stopped.

The number of years when time did not stop.

The number of your last year.

Not the number of mine.

The number of your year you died when someone blew you up. Or rather, you allowed yourself to be blown up. Even in death teaching lessons.

The number of my year I begin teaching creative writing. On your anniversary, I wonder what you would be doing. You'd be fifty-one. Ten more than what you were given. Bee Sting told me that you told him you were retiring after that pump. At forty-one, the age you almost made it to and the age I am.

Four and one. 4 + 1. 5. Five, the age my son first met you. He hung on your arm at that family brief, remember? You shook my hand. You said I had some grit. To my handshake and for coming to meet my new Sergeant Major. My son swung around you like monkey bars in a sandbox. Monkey bars. Tall and made of iron. You. Tall and made of iron. My son, five, four plus one, hung from you and swung from you, around you as you sized me up. Later you'd call me a good piece of gear. High praise.

The number of your year you never saw your daughter again.

I wonder how old she is, what she does now, what milestones you've missed.

The number of my year that I fly to California to watch my son in his eighteenth year graduate from boot camp. I would have invited you, Sergeant Major Ellis (ret.). My son would have remembered you.

The number of my year that I sit in an auditorium listening to parents cheer when the Marine Corps Family Team Building lady says, No retreat, No surrender, or some other bumper sticker bullshit. The number of my year I get angry at those parents for not realizing that they are cheering for a folded flag, an SGLI payment, an end of years, and a brother counting years.

HURRY UP AND WAIT

To the man who checked me into my hotel,
It gets better. It gets easier.
Skeptical, he asks when.

After a while, I say.
I don't say a while is open-ended, ambiguous, nebulous, mysterious
like being alive after a combat deployment when he isn't when she
isn't when they aren't. I don't say that because he has the look.

That look. I've seen that look, know that look, had that look.

That when does transition happen when does it get easier does it get
easier is it always gonna be like this broke and angry and impatient I
wasn't scared just scared and tired and hungry sometimes and now
I'm not scared just scared and tired and angry when I'm hungry I
don't fit in when I try I am acting copying what I see other people
do and I wouldn't say I'm alone but I'm so alone because dead baby
jokes are funny and so is canoeing a guy's head but not shooting
dogs and I don't know these civilians by sight in the dark or what
the sound of their breathing is like while I am on post so they can
sleep or what their kids' names are and they don't ask anything about
me because dead baby jokes are funny and so is canoeing a guy's
head and we speak English but not the same language so when do

I transition they say I have to transition I'm not transitioning but if maybe the GI Bill money would kick in so I could get a haircut and put food on the table and get an education and a job this will get easier when does it get easier does it get easier look.

Yeah. That look. I know that look, had that look. Have that look sometimes. Still.

Still, it does get easier, gets better. He is suspicious. In boot camp during the dark days a recruit ahead of us whispers it in MOS school in the lonely days the restricted libo days no civvies days someone senior than us by a month or so would say it. We would believe it. And it never did get better. But it did. Field ops and rain drops and transpo not coming and hurry up and wait and tired and dirty and laughing and smoking and dipping and cussing and humping and firing and connecting. It got better. It did not get better. The boredom the separation the boredom the mortars the boredom the small arms the boredom the IEDs the boredom the close calls the packing up your buddy's gear to send home the dirt and smell of ass of feet of armpit of ball sweat of shit of blood of dead body the boredom that not even a CONEX box of baby wipes can wipe away. It did get better. The smokes, dip, fresh cammies, hot chow, hot coffee, a shower, a few hours of uninterrupted sleep. The laughter, the tears, the jokes, the silences. The trip home, the memorial services, the leave, the boredom, the disconnection, the silence, the empty, the quiet, the dead, the desire. To live. Again. It gets better.

After the winter, the frail brown skeletal stretching branches of a hydrangea show green buds, tiny, tiny, tiny bits of green that you have to focus to see, a hint of the magic the mystery of the cycle against the painted white-gray wall on the shed of the house you buy years after. Every day you walk outside and breathe the air and feel the air on your face and the green buds get bigger, better. Leaves. Soon flowers.

It gets better just like that, brother who checked me into my hotel for a writing conference I am attending as a faculty member at a university—me a faculty member, me! The loud, brown working-class kid with a smart mouth and a belligerent attitude who once made a man cry from rage okay, twice, two men, and almost killed a child that could have been a threat who laughs at dead baby jokes and canoeing a guy's head. Me. A writer. Me. A temp faculty member attending a writer's conference so far away from field ops and rain drops and transpo not coming and hurry up and wait and tired and dirty and laughing and smoking and dipping and cussing and humping and boredom and separation and mortars and small arms and close calls and dirt and smell of ass of feet of armpit of ball sweat of shit of blood of dead body and the joy of fresh cammies, hot chow, hot coffee, a shower, a few hours of uninterrupted sleep and laughter and tears and jokes and silences and yet right next to all of that. Me. And you. Us. Standing. Together. Hurrying up. Waiting.

TIME

The waves crash and retreat against the shore of Masonboro Island. A young Iraq vet watches the waves, the surfers, the birds. He says nothing. He thinks about the all the times he sat in front of the ocean on the West Coast. How he waited for answers. How he waited for emotions to come rolling in with the next wave. Nothing ever came.

A divorce, a move, and some years later he now sits on the beach facing the Atlantic. Waiting. Listening. He remembers the beaches of California. He remembers the sand of Iraq. He leans against his backpack like he used to lean against his pack. He adjusts his ball cap to cover his eyes. He smiles. Old habits are hard to break, he says. I can fall asleep anywhere, he says. He settles in and naps.

Behind the Iraq vet and just to the right a Vietnam vet paints in silence while the Iraq vets sleeps. The Vietnam vet paints a scene of the shore across the channel. With careful, deliberate brushstrokes, he paints.

The waves crash and pelicans dip. The Iraq vet wakes because he senses movement to his left. He sits up adjusts his ball cap, looks around. He has not felt this refreshed in years. He thinks it is good to be there in the sand on the beach with the sun warming him.

Then the Iraq vet kneels in front of his backpack. He takes his cigar case from the backpack. The Iraq vet likes cigars. The Iraq vet unwraps one of two cigars in the case. He cuts it. He lights it. Puffs the cigar and smiles. He walks up to the older Vietnam vet's left side and stops a few feet from him. He draws on his cigar. The Vietnam vet never speaks of Vietnam. The Iraq vet always speaks of Iraq.

The Iraq vet watches the Vietnam vet paint. Minutes pass. Pelicans in formation fly along the waves tops, sand crabs skitter into holes. The wind blows. The Iraq vet stands. The Vietnam vet paints.

The Iraq vet steps toward the Vietnam vet. He stops just behind the Vietnam vet's left shoulder. Does it just take time, the Iraq vet says, looking at the shore that does not look like the painting.

Yes, it does take time, the Vietnam vet says. He brushes green onto a shrub.

Am I in your light, the Iraq vet says.

No, that helps. The sun dries the paint, the Vietnam vet says. He finishes a yellow beach. But your eyes don't adjust to the shadow, he says. It's a balance, the Vietnam vet says.

The Vietnam vet does not look at the Iraq vet. He looks at the shore. He looks at his canvas. He looks at his paint. He looks back at the shore. He dabs more blue for the sea. The thing to remember is you don't have to paint exactly what you see, he says to the Iraq vet. You can use it, but you don't have to get it all.

BOOTS, REVISITED

I threw my combat boots away on a random Thursday afternoon after keeping them in a closet, in a bag stowed in a footlocker, for eleven years after I got out. The ones I deployed in, the ones I kept under my desk at the Naval Academy, the ones I wrote an essay about. The ones with my dog tag in the left boot, caked in Iraqi sand and Okinawan clay, the earth of all the places in between. The suede rubbed bare, the soles flat. The ones I kept for memory, for fear of letting go.

When I threw them out I was cleaning up the office closet my footlocker is in for my son, who when he was a toddler was there to see me off to Iraq, who shouted cool and rushed at me to grab my rifle and bayonet, whom I kept a picture of in my helmet, who would send me boxes when I was in Iraq filled with snacks and a letter and maybe a drawing, who would draw me with an angry face killing bad guys when I came home, who would pretend to clear our house like I'd shown him, who'd told me over a cup of hot chocolate in front of the reptile house at the San Diego Zoo that he would treat my divorce from his mom like a deployment, who as I teared up from telling him I was leaving him told me not to cry as he blinked back his own tears because he would be fine because lots of his friends' parents were divorced and it was kinda normal, who would tell me years later he wanted to join the Marines, who would join the Young Marines and I would pin his meritorious rank on and teach him to march and polish his boots like I used to, who would join the real Marines as a grunt, who would get stationed in my old regiment at my old camp and eat at the chow hall I used to and would run all the old trails I ran, who had gotten out of the Marines and needed some space to hang his and his wife's clothes since they moved home to my house.

I wish I had a cooler story than that. One like you might see in a war movie where the broken and war-torn war vet has this moment where he stares off into space and a montage of the war and the after plays like a flashback and the music manipulates the crowd's emotions so you know how hard it was for the war vet to part with something he held on to for so long and maybe the war vet would wipe a small tear and smile a half smile and shake his head and hold on to those boots that he knows so well, boots that even know him and how his feet should sit in them and where he has walked and how many miles and the places he's been and what he thought and felt and all the memorial services and parades and tears and laughs, and the camera would zoom in and maybe there would be a cool sunset to hammer home the point he was ready, that he had made peace with his past and his demons, and then he would say something stupid like farewell old friends or touch them one last loving time before he tossed or placed them in a trash can depending on what the director and actor playing a war vet thought best and most authentic in that moment or maybe all of that but add that the war vet's kid who is now also a vet walks in and watches from afar or maybe speaks to his war vet dad and they embrace and some cool poignant thing happens and we know that the war vet is healed and the credits roll.

But the truth is I don't have a cool story like that, or a soundtrack to my life, though a soundtrack would be kind of cool, and my kid who is a man and a vet doesn't even know that I threw my combat boots away and why would I tell him since it wasn't a big deal or that I cut the boot laces like a casualty's to remove my dog tag from my left boot and then tossed the boots in the kitchen trash on top of used coffee grounds and other garbage and then took the bag outside because the trash was full and went back to making room in my office closet for my son and his wife. It was a Thursday. It was late afternoon. I was home alone. We needed the space.

SOMETIMES

Sometimes it's homesickness for coming home after work to everyone you know and who knows you and who matters most to you in the world standing on the catwalk in T-shirts and silkies and flip-flops as boots get hazed and alcohol gets consumed in dangerous large quantities or for that time that you had to go on a sixteen-mile patrol to contact which is a little more intense than just a walk with a seventy-pound ruck and being tired as shit and boy did that fucking suck but then laughing after over a beer or twenty and maybe going out to get laid but instead getting so drunk that you had to run from the cops and then try to figure out a way to get past PMO at the gate because they are a bunch of buddy fuckers and now that those guys are gone you notice that you don't laugh so much and you can still hear their voices but they've moved on gotten married gotten out or died and you just wish sometimes you could tell them you love them and miss them and then saying no homo after so they don't fuck with you even though you know they feel the same

And sometimes it's fear that nothing will ever be the same because your world was in that squad platoon company battalion and maybe you didn't like everyone but goddam would you kill a lot of motherfuckers for them and now it's gone and you don't understand the civilian lack of responsibility or accountability or courtesy or practical fucking sense or the civilian inability to be a man of his word or the fact that no one moves with a fucking purpose at all out here and it maddens you to no end but what can you do so you keep your hands in your pockets so you don't choke slam someone for saying stupid shit like what was it like to kill someone or I wish I had free college or I almost joined or I know someone who joined do you know him or you just have to move past all that PTSD stuff or I always thought people joined the military because they had no future or you can't kill an ideology or I support the troops or you don't look disabled and [my favorite] I understand what you're going through because I played Call of Duty or watched *American Sniper* or read about it in some book but they don't know anything about it because they don't know what it's like to feel the ground shake from an explosion or how you go deaf for a minute or so or how loud our weapons really are and the snap of a bullet as it goes by your head and so you keep your hands in your pockets and your mouth shut but it does nothing for the rage and when will it go away and maybe it isn't even the civilians' fault that they don't know not to say stupid shit you just wish they would stop talking to you because you don't want to hear them run their mouths about how hard or stressful something is and you hate when people ask you what war was like because how do you answer that in a socially acceptable sentence or two which is all the time they have to pay attention and listen and you hate being angry at people for doing things that they don't know piss you off and you aren't even sure why it pisses you off just that it does so instead of lashing out you withdraw and stop talking to people and then your wife or girlfriend notices that you are closed off and don't talk as much as you once did and you don't laugh or smile hardly ever at all anymore

And sometimes it's just missing people who say things like how's your gay porn career and you answer I dunno I've been busy fucking your mother and someone says how wonderful it is to be around a bunch of people who aren't such a bunch of sensitive bitches who think things like heads smashed by bullets and terrorists detonating themselves or watching fast movers unleash hell on some goat fucker is funny because it is because how else are you supposed to react when people have tried to kill you and your friends and you and they survived and hey everything else is a big joke because you lived and Haji or goat fucker or whatever else you call him didn't and the stress was so great that if you didn't laugh you might cry and not that there is anything wrong with crying because you have cried plenty and so have your friends but only alone or maybe together but never in front of outsiders because that's what everyone else is outsiders even your spouse because they have never known how exhilarating it is to survive someone's failure to kill you

And sometimes it's wondering when you'll wake from the dream the fantasy because it's just not possible to be back to be alive to be wearing civilian clothes civilian shoes but still feeling like you're in boots and cammies or flak and Kevlar and no matter what this can't be real it isn't real because it's almost too good to be true and if it is then it isn't but it isn't too good because you don't think it's real and so you go through the motions and your wife begs you to come back but you don't know where you are how you got there or how to get back and do you even want to come back what if you want to stay in this world where your friends—no, this is the new reality it just takes getting used to and you fake it till you make it and pretend to be engaged even though you're dis-

And other times you're doing fine and you aren't angry and you aren't sad and you're driving along a road and you see a Muslim wearing manjammies talking on a cellphone and cars form a choke-point and a woman in hijab pulls in front of you and stops her car and your butthole tightens and you reach for a rifle that isn't there and you feel the weight of a flak and Kevlar you aren't wearing because you forget you're in America and everyone has cellphones and you realize they are Americans just going about their day like you are and they aren't trying to kill you

And sometimes you're doing fine and you aren't angry and you aren't sad but you still aren't connecting to civilians but you kind of are and you still sit in a corner watching the exits but you're trying and it's getting better but then you see a movie that has nothing to do with war only it has everything to do with war and you start to shake and you start to sweat but you gut it out and talk to the civilians around you about it and they say they've learned something and you realize you can get past this and maybe just maybe civilians aren't so bad

And sometimes you can be sitting on the couch in your living room and it's not even someone's death anniversary but you see something on TV that has to do with the war but usually it has nothing to do with the war and you get choked up because civilians read a headline or hear about a soldier who was wounded or killed and they never know the actual cost that someone's voice is forever silent that you aren't ever gonna see that smartass grin and it's just so hard the knowing what it costs as you sit on the couch all choked up in clean clothes in your house when so many folks aren't but then someone says what did it cost and you get even more frustrated because they don't understand and you don't understand why they don't under-stand until you realize that nothing here has value because we have 500 brands of cereal and unlimited froufrou coffee and cars and food and no one has ever had to give up anything of real value and no one is really willing to fight for anything as far as you can tell but then you get frustrated because you try to explain it and you just sound arrogant so you get more frustrated but you aren't trying to be an asshole you just want people to realize how great we have it here and how you think people get wrapped around the axle when they have everything but the more you talk the worse it gets so you just stop trying to explain it

And sometimes people expect you to be antiwar now since you sur-vived and are in a creative writing department but you aren't antiwar in fact you believe in war because you've seen what it can do for peo-ple like that guy with no ears or those little girls who can go to school even though you know how much it costs and not just the bullets and beans and bandages but the reality of it like not going to church anymore because maybe God stopped speaking to you or maybe he never spoke at all and that first marriage and the bad dreams and all the rest of it that you would do it again to give those people over there a chance at life and if it meant the terrorists went there to fight us instead of attacking our home it was worth the cost even if people back home don't see it that way and questions like are the Iraqis and Afghans better off after the long war are useless to discuss because being prowar or at least not antiwar is unpopular and not complicated enough and that is what people will never understand about why we want to go back because of how uncomplicated it was because you couldn't control if you got hit you just tried to make sure you didn't but if you did you did and back here there's mortgages and bills and people think they rate opinions on things they don't rate opinions on and hey aren't you an elitist because you think people should stay in their fucking lane and you are so angry but you aren't really just confused because why do people talk about stuff they know nothing about and why do people get so spun up when we have everything because even our poor are living in luxury compared to the poverty you've seen

And sometimes even though you think you're numb you aren't in some ways because you've seen real suffering but you just sometimes think civilian suffering is whining even though it isn't always just whining though it can be because no one mutilates little girls' genitals here and no one sneaks into your house at night to kidnap and torture or decapitate you and you don't have a dirt floor in your house and even though when people die of natural causes or because they overdosed or just had an accident and people get all worked up over it you try to be as gentle as you can because you know how much that shit hurts and so you realize you aren't numb that you do care about the civilians around you and that if you could spare them the pain you've lived or help them along you would but it just comes off as numb because maybe you are starting to care again but you don't want to get hurt if you let your guard down and someone gets hurt so maybe that's part of the reason you stay vigilant and people maybe make jokes about you behind your back but that's fine because you know you'll react if you can and try to save the random civilians around you because that is who you are

And sometimes the days are bad and sure maybe you're sad or angry because if you don't eat you get angry because your body remembers not eating meant war and war meant violence and anger and the threat of death so you keep snacks around to keep the anger at bay

And sometimes you don't even like vets because they are all thank me for my service and give me free shit or discounted shit and you're like we volunteered so maybe just give us some space and not things because free meals and discounts don't have to mean appreciation and support as much as a kind word or touch on the shoulder to show that maybe the civilian doesn't understand but that they kind of sort of in their own way care

And sometimes you notice the bad days are fewer and farther between

And sometimes when you wake in the morning even though you still remember standing to and how quiet the desert was and how beautiful the stars were you notice that the day is beautiful and the sky is blue and today is okay and eventually today becomes two days and okay becomes not bad and maybe just maybe not bad becomes good again and then maybe we scare ourselves and chastise ourselves because we are comfortable and it isn't so bad because what if we forget which is why we have RED Friday for remembering everyone deployed but we aren't ever going to forget and we remember that we are warriors not victims so maybe today we start walking like a warrior with our head up and our chest out and we start helping our community and giving back like those times we did COMRELS because giving is what life is all about and if we needed proof we could just look at the bracelet on our wrist or in our memories and our dead friends will tell us it's fine that they know we love them and they aren't leaving and we won't forget and maybe if we talk more about some of the things but not all of them people will start to understand and maybe we should focus on the now like we did in country so we don't miss anything.

HIP-POCKET LECTURER

I couldn't walk on the grass my first semester as an undergrad student. Not just wouldn't. Couldn't. And I judged the fuck out of the normies who sat on the grass, walked on the grass, oblivious to the impending doom in the form of a screaming First Sergeant that walking on the grass brings even though I was a little jealous that they didn't have to unlearn stupid shit like that.

We aren't allowed to walk on the grass in the military. The Navy and Marine Corps have this sick fascination with grass, though in my experience the "grass" was always some shitty piece of dirt with a few wisps of yellow, fibrous plant matter that always "belonged" to some senior Marine and some poor PFC or Lance Corporal had to maintain it.

The no walking on the grass thing is so strong that once in Sydney, Australia, coming home from Iraq, we had to cross Hyde Park to go down toward King's Cross. Simple enough, right? There was only grass on this park and one ribbon of concrete bisecting the park. The concrete went in the opposite direction that we needed to go. The woman with us stepped off the concrete and about five paces in noticed we hadn't followed. She looked over her shoulder to see that we (me, Bear, Turbo, Little Montalvo, and Wee Man) were all of us stopped on the concrete looking at the grass like we were at the edge of some terrifying cliff. She asked what the problem was, and we said we can't walk on the grass. You big bad Marine combat vets can't walk on the grass? That's fucking stupid, she said. You don't understand, we said. We looked at Bear. He said fuck it, we look stupid. And walking all the way north to turn and walk down the other sidewalk was stupid. So, we all in unison took one step into the grass and we didn't die. You'd have thought we were crossing into enemy territory the way we felt, but I digress.

I'd gotten out of the Navy on a Monday, drove from Annapolis down to Camp Lejeune with a trunk full of my stuff, and started school on Thursday the same week. My new peers were the same age as my boots. I was the same age as most of my professors. I was thirty-four years old. And I couldn't walk on the grass.

My first class that Thursday was at 8:00 a.m. CRW 201 Intro to Creative Writing, a class that I wasn't even sure I wanted to take. But I had a gap in my schedule, and the VA rules for the GI Bill said I needed to fill it, so I figured why the fuck not. My second week of class, I walked into our classroom, which was still dark, and something with a sharp object in its hand jumped out at me. I turned to kill the threat only to hear Alison, my TA, say, Michael! She was turning on the light when I walked in and had a handful of colored pencils for a writing exercise she wanted us to do. I apologized. She apologized. I was sure she was going to report the crazy vet who almost killed her. She didn't.

I wrote some poems and a short story in that class. My fellow students didn't like my poem about the pajama people and their lack of hygiene. I couldn't figure out why students couldn't wear real clothes to class, show up on time, or shower regularly, but I was the weirdo because I wrote about Iraq.

Alison asked what my major was, what my plans were, and I said history and foreign languages so I could apply for a commission in the Marine Corps and go to Afghanistan since I had already been to Iraq. She told me I should take another creative writing class. I had some space in my schedule, so I took another one my second semester, CRW 209, Intro to Creative Nonfiction.

The first nonfiction piece I ever wrote was "Boxes," and the *Sun* published it in Readers Write. I didn't think my essay was very good and I worried that the *Sun* only picked it because I was a war vet, and they wanted a story from a vet. At the same time the *Sun* published my essay, the Navy enlisted and Marine officer recruiters told me thank you for your service but you can't come back in. Josh, my TA in CRW 209, had been trying to convince me I was supposed to be a writer. I guess he was right.

I didn't know what to do when the Navy and Marine Corps told me thanks but no thanks. I had only ever wanted to continue to do what I was good at, going to war. But since that wasn't an option, I did what I knew. The Marine Corps taught me that I was supposed to be the very best at what I did, otherwise what was the point of doing it? So, I learned to write sentences and paragraphs that functioned together like our weapon systems. I learned to use words and white space like we use tactics to take an objective, to hold the objective, combined arms only with words and rhythm and image. My objective wasn't terrain or protecting a chaplain, it was telling the stories of my brothers, my story. Most of the guys I know, they wouldn't ever tell their stories to folks at home. But I thought if I got good at writing, and I tell my story and by extension theirs, maybe people will know what my Marines and sailors were like. How good and funny and irreverent and brave and strong and human they were.

I think that's why the poor, poor me vet story irritates me so much. Do some people struggle? Yes. Are those vets the majority? No. The government invested a lot of money in us and in making us resilient and adaptable and strong and successful. They taught us how not to quit or fail. And so many of us are out here raising our families, holding down jobs, taking the good our service has taught us and using it to better our communities. But all people want to hear is how messed up we are. How monstrous we are. How detached. How broken. I don't understand why. And I don't understand why my story has to be what someone else expects.

But I also hate the hero narrative. You know the one, the conservative American who loves Jesus and killed all the infidels with an American flag on his back and his boot on the neck of some enemy of America who is now home and fighting the liberal onslaught. Save it. The vast majority of us were not trigger pullers, just regular people who did the job asked of us, and we just want to be treated like people. To be valued. To be heard. Or to be left alone.

I had a professor, Sarah Messer, who told me that she was, of course, antiwar and anti-Bush and though my writing didn't change her views, I did remind her that the people who fought are people with moms and dads and sisters like her sister. She told me I personalized the war and what happens after in a way she wasn't prepared for, and I wasn't telling the same old stories in the same old ways. For me that was the point. The turning point even. What am I saying that hasn't already been said?

Humans have been telling war stories since forever. *Epic of Gilgamesh. The Iliad.* Hardly anyone ever talks about the after, and that's what I am most interested in. What happens after the war? How do you take all those skills you learned in the military, in a war zone, and apply them to everyday life? Because they apply, believe it or not.

Another professor, Wendy Brenner, told me that war veterans aren't the only ones with a monopoly on suffering. She was right. People are people and we all hurt the same and I wasn't prepared for that. The first breakup, or the rich kid with a pill problem? The student who lost a parent or a friend, a classmate? Maybe the circumstances are different, but the grief and pain are the same as mine. David Gessner, another professor and a friend, said that the essay I wrote about sleep and nightmares resonated with him because he had an accident when he was younger and even now all those years later, he still has the occasional nightmare.

Wendy also showed me the Archer films and I realized that *A Matter of Life and Death* was a war film, and from the Archers I learned about texture and color and art making us whole and being the only thing worth fighting for.

Marines love to fight. Marines also love to teach. Did you know that? Ask a Marine about a weapon, a tactic, a radio, how to call for fire or call for air, how to be a coxswain, how to broach a boat, when to use a donut charge or a hydrostatic charge, anything, and you will get a hip-pocket class on it. They even teach a class on how to teach a class. Hip-pocket lectures, we call them. And it will be the best class you ever had. I don't think they know this, but teaching is an act of service. Of love. You want to pass on your knowledge so that your student lives to fight and see another day. Being Greenside Navy, I acquired the same love of teaching. So, when my university offered a graduate TA-ship in creative writing on top of offering me a spot in their graduate program, I was stoked.

When I would tell my Marine friends that I was a writer they were stoked for me. When I told them I was a graduate teaching assistant, that I taught undergrads creative writing, they couldn't believe it. They didn't know who thought it would be a good idea to put me in front of civilian kids, but they all asked if they could come visit and watch the fun. The fun being me lighting into a bunch of undisciplined, whiny civilian kids. My friends knew me as a fire-breather, a hard-ass, and they were proud of me. They should be because they taught me.

My first lesson was in late '02, at Mateo on Pendleton, after I pinned on Third Class Petty Officer, with Shouse, Turbo, and Stover. I had asked why when they walked anywhere Marines got out of their way, respected them, talked to them with a healthy fear and reverence but ignored me. We all walked to PAC. They told me to walk in and they watched me. After watching me stop and move to the side, say excuse me and stop again, they told me that I didn't walk with confidence, with the rank I wore, that the Marines could sense my politeness, which they read as fear, and exploited it. Shouse, Turbo, and Stover told me to walk through again, only this time keep my head up and not give the other Marines the road. No, they'd say, do it again when I stopped or said excuse me. We did it again and again until the junior Marines got out of my way, and then we did it more until that confidence was a part of me. Leading PT, close-order drill, giving hip-pocket lectures on anything and everything, they looked out for me, taught me how to be assertive and aggressive. I overcame my fear and overpoliteness. I knew then I could do anything.

As a faculty member, I once taught four of our department's Graduate Teaching Assistants, Cassie, Tory, Lindsay, and Cass, how to clear rooms. I put them in the stack and taught them how to get set, to squeeze the shoulder of the person in front of them when ready, to move fluidly through the door, to pie the room, how their eyes should follow their weapons—hands in this case—how to say clear and regroup and move to the next room and the next. I taught them that if this was real, there was a chance one of them could die, that fire superiority was the best medicine, that they'd have to move whichever of them got hit out of the line of fire for a Doc to treat while they kept pushing to the objective. I taught them that slow is smooth and smooth is fast. I taught them that amateurs do it until they get it right but professionals do it until they can't get it wrong. I taught them the value of muscle memory and repetition and confidence. I taught them how to settle the adrenaline and anxiety and to do the task at hand. I taught them they can do anything even when they think they can't.

When the pandemic hit, right before we all got kicked off campus, I told my undergrads that this might sound weird or intrusive but that we were all going to be told to go home and stay home. That we couldn't interact with people. That days on end of isolation and boredom would be unhealthy for us as social animals. I said that to stay sane they needed to get up every day, make their beds, shower and brush their teeth, get dressed in real clothes, establish a routine. That that routine, that discipline would help build resilience and mental strength and get them through the dark times. They listened. A few of those students thanked me later and said that my advice saved them.

I am glad it did. Because some people didn't have that support and they didn't make it. Rory Hamil, a vet a lot of us in the vet community knew, killed himself pretty early on in the isolation period. That sucked. Losing someone always does. I didn't want to see the same thing happen to any of the kids I was responsible for teaching.

I was talking with Bear a few years back and we were talking about how people say being a war vet makes you numb and care less about people and that that isn't always true. He found, and I have, too, that our experiences made us care more for folks and feel more deeply in some ways. The word is empathy. We are more empathetic because of our experiences.

We know what loss is like. We know what it is to never hear your friend's laugh again or see him do Edward Forty Hands again. We have seen civilians who just wanted to live a normal life like us— moms, dads, sisters, brothers like us, like ours—suffer because they live in a country our government decided we are at war with.

We know what joy is like. And laughter. The best belly laughs I ever had, the best meals, the best times. The only difference is, when my service was over everyone told me I had to forget all of that. That I had to transition, that I had to find a new identity.

Fuck that.

My students. Almost all of them introduce themselves to me over email. Like I don't know who they are. As if they barely exist in a class of twelve to nineteen students. They feel invisible. Undervalued. Misheard or ignored. It's heartbreaking that your polite civilian world, the one I don't fit in, the one that doesn't want to hear my story because it isn't easily marketable or digestible, makes its children feel anonymous. But I should change and be more like that? No thanks.

They say sorry a lot, too, my students. Sorry for disagreeing, sorry for talking, sorry for needing to get by me in a hallway. Sorry. I tell my students that I don't want their apology. In fact, they shouldn't apologize for disagreeing or having a different opinion, for being human, for taking up space in the world. The civilian world taught them that. The one that wants me to conform to it. Marine Corps leadership taught me to be confident and competent and humble enough to apologize for my mistakes but never for my existence.

Marine leaders eat last. And sometimes, leaders serve their Marines chow. Did you know that? Do you know why? Because the job of leadership is to make sure that the folks who are doing the fighting and the dying, the work, that their needs are met before anyone else's. It's the same reason they get to know their Marines. How can you lead people if you don't know what motivates them, what they worry about, what excites them? How can you lead them if you aren't willing to serve them?

When I was NCOIC of the S-1 in Oki we went to Subic Bay for libo. Part of my responsibility was making the shore patrol watch bill and my First Sergeant, First Sergeant Carlson, the one with the Suicide Charley tattoo on his left forearm that was bigger than my thigh, who told me his dick was shrinking because he left the grunts to work in admin, told me not to be afraid to put myself on that watch bill, to give my Marines a break. He was right.

During the pandemic when the PubLab TAs I led had yet another last-minute design job that needed to get done and I could tell they were doing everything they could just to hold themselves together, I did it myself. My TAs were relieved. Later, Cassie, one of the ones I taught how to clear a room, asked me why I stepped in then and from time to time to take the work from them, and I told her the story about the watch bill.

This is why I get angry when people tell me I am useless. That my military career and the skills I learned there are useless here. That's why I get angry at vets who buy into the lie that we can't serve still.

And you know what's funny? Most of my colleagues don't make me feel that way. They accept me for me and what I bring to the table. It hasn't been a rose garden. I once had a fellow faculty member tell all of us, me included, that only they knew what it was like to be in enemy territory. No, they were not a war veteran. It just so happened they said this on Veterans Day, talk about timing.

So when vets and civilians ask me how I made it, I tell them the truth. I smiled and waved. I bit my tongue until it bled. I didn't hold my tongue. I did strike back after perceived attacks. I stayed true to my culture and my Marines and myself. That I am not sorry or repentant for serving or whatever the fuck it is I supposedly have done in Iraq. And I continue to serve. I recognize that people are people, and we all want to be heard. Whether that is an undergrad finding their voice for the first time or a graduate student taking a creative risk or a vet who isn't a hero or a victim just trying to tell their story their way. We are the same. And I try to remember that.

ACKNOWLEDGMENTS

I don't want this to turn into an overlong Oscars speech, but so many people had a hand in helping this book exist that I fear it might, but I don't want to leave anyone out either.

Thank you to my son, Michael, daughter, Morgan, and wife, Lisa, one of the strongest female vets I know, for putting up with my choice of profession in the After.

Thank you to the *Sun*, *Fourth Genre*, and *Press Pause* for publishing "Boxes," "A Long and Incomplete List," and "Hearsay."

Thank you to Cate Hodorowicz, my editor at UNC Press, for listening to a cranky old vet talk about his book and for deciding it was a worthwhile project.

Thank you to the staff at UNC Press for making this book. I know full well bringing a book into the world isn't just the work of a writer. Also, typesetting this must have been a nightmare, so thanks for your patience.

Thank you to my friends and colleagues in the Department of Creative Writing at UNC Wilmington for always asking me when my book was going to get published, for your time, generosity, mentorship, fellowship, the laughs, the hard lessons, and the banh mi.

Special thanks to Philip Gerard. Without you this book would not have happened and I miss you very much.

To the PubLab Tas—you know who you are—thank you for letting me lead you, for trusting me, and being the best team I could have ever asked for on this side of the bang.

Thanks to my students for always indulging me and listening to me talk about writing, publishing, book design, leadership, and anything else that comes to mind.

Thank you to the OAF crew of writers that I worked with for always being receptive to my edits and ideas and just being solid folks.

Thanks to the DRC crew for publishing and championing veteran writers, pushing veteran writing communities, and letting me help out when I could.

Thanks to Kacey Tellesen, Aaron Kirk, Graham Barnhart, and John Dailey, fellow veteran writers I know and respect and whose work has had such an influence on me, and for just being solid dudes.

Thanks to Tim O'Brien for telling me it was never safe to be vulnerable but that I owed it to my guys to tell my story and to tell theirs.

Thanks to Karl Marlantes for telling me I was right, that you can see mortars at the top of their arc, and for being an example of growth and generosity as a writer and veteran and for the taco soup.

But really, the largest thanks, and biggest debt I owe is to the Marines and sailors of 1st CEB and 2/4, of 1 MARDIV, and everywhere in between that I served with, deployed with, drank with, and talked about the After with. I have learned so much from you about service, honor, duty, dedication, camaraderie, leadership, and the list can go on. Thanks for always having my six and letting me tag along, with love, your RP.